Library of Congress Cataloging-in-Publication Data

Hess, Alan.
    Viva Las Vegas: After-Hours Architecture / by Alan Hess
       p. cm.
    Filmography: p. 127
    Includes bibliographical references and index.
    ISBN 0-8118-0111-X
    1. Architecture—Nevada—Las Vegas—Themes, Motives.
    2. Las Vegas (Nev.)—Buildings, structures, etc. I. Title.
    NA735.L37H47 1993
    720'.9793'135—dc20
92-39642
CIP

Printed in Japan.
Distributed in Canada by
Raincoast Books
112 East Third Avenue
Vancouver, B.C. V5T 1C8

10 9 8 7 6 5 4 3 2 1

Chronicle Books
275 Fifth Street
San Francisco, CA 94103

PHOTO CREDITS

Chicago Art Institute
Del Webb Corporation
Las Vegas News Bureau
The Luckman Partnership
Nevada Historical Society
University of Nevada, Las Vegas, Special Collections
John English Collection
Jim Heimann Collection
Alan Hess Collection
Donn Knepp Collection
Harris Sharp Collection
Hugh Taylor Collection
Kermit Wayne Collection

♠ ♦ ♣ ♥

VIVA LAS VEGAS

After-Hours Architecture

ALAN HESS

FOREWORD BY
ROBERT VENTURI, DENISE SCOTT BROWN,
AND STEVEN IZENOUR

CHRONICLE BOOKS
SAN FRANCISCO

For I., always in my heart.

Contents

Las Vegas—
Learning to understand,
and even love,
what we love to hate.

"EAT, GAS, EXIT, FREE ASPIRIN, ASK US ANYTHING, WELCOME TO LAS VEGAS."

In September 1968 the three of us and fifteen Yale University graduate students were welcomed to Las Vegas by these signs and a headline in the *Las Vegas Sun*, "Yale Professor Agrees to Praise Strip for $5,000." Reading Alan Hess's evocative history of our own Xanadu in the desert, it seems obvious that Las Vegas is still a city in the sand where yesterday's hype and dream become tomorrow's fantastic reality.

Las Vegas was once a humble watering stop on the Southern Pacific Railroad line but, owing to its geography and to some aspects of human nature, it became a hugely successful resort and oasis. The city is the extreme example of two American urban themes, the gridiron plan and the automobile strip.

We went to the Southwest because we wanted to learn about new forms of urbanism. We chose Las Vegas for study because it had the biggest, brightest strip in the world and we were interested in learning about an architecture of color, decoration, signs, and symbols—an architecture people seemed to enjoy more than what we serious architects were offering them. Where better to see the classic elements of roadside architecture than in Las Vegas, where signs are more important then buildings? As the *Sun* headline pointed out, our time and resources were limited. In *Learning from Las Vegas*, we were able only to scratch the surface of the social, economic, architectural, and anecdotal history, whose tapestry has now been filled in by Alan Hess.

A quarter century ago, few design professionals or scholarly observers took Las Vegas seriously; the city's laissez-faire attitudes toward architecture, signs, and glitter represented all that designers of good taste loved to hate. Twenty-four years later Las Vegas is still derided as a symbol of excess. Therefore, what can a not-so-ancient history of Las Vegas teach us today?

It can point to the need for sensitive observation and analysis of what is and how it got that way, before we embark on grand schemes for improving the American city or suburb. *Viva Las Vegas* suggests that large-scale, complex physical environments like Las Vegas should be examined open-mindedly, and from political, economic, symbolic, and historical as well as formal perspectives

The book teaches that not all aspects of the environment are amenable to the tender touch of architectural "good taste" or to the ministrations of the ubiquitous fine arts commissions; that it is often preferable to accept and glorify in the pluralism of the Good, the Bad, and the Ugly than to enforce the white bread dullness of good taste all over the landscape; and that we can try to change our everyday surroundings by design, or we can work to perhaps more profound effect in the city by learning to see the commonplace through new eyes.

In other words, let's learn to understand, love, and even laugh with what we thought we hated. Long live the big sign and the little building! Long live the building that is a sign! Long live Las Vegas!

ROBERT VENTURI
DENISE SCOTT BROWN
STEVEN IZENOUR

The Strip was not much to look at by day. Flat and two-dimensional.
An idiot Disneyland of architectural parabolas, overloaded utility poles, celestial hamburger stands
and gimcrackery fairy palaces. Wait until you see it at night, I was told.
At night it was an idiot Disneyland with lights.

JOHN GREGORY DUNNE, **VEGAS: A MEMOIR OF A DARK SEASON**, 1974

Introduction

LAS VEGAS AND DISNEYLAND are the two most potent urban models in twentieth-century America. This is a book about Las Vegas.

In the nineteenth century hamlets along railroad tracks burgeoned into gridiron cities focused on the train station. Today we see similar growth in lowrise suburbs along car-oriented commercial strips blossoming into linear cities with highrise towers, dense populations, and social centers. The Las Vegas Strip, a three-and-a-half-mile highway south of the city limits, is the ultimate version of the commercial strips found on the fringes of almost all American cities. Without question, the Strip is an exaggerated example. It is a resort, not an ordinary city. But it offers a way to study the compelling phenomenon of these populist, sprawling, postindustrial cities. These days, Las Vegas no longer seems like an anomaly.

Like other towns, Las Vegas began with a traditional Main Street, Fremont Street, with sidewalks and storefronts. The alternative city center that blossomed along the Strip, however, looks nothing like that traditional downtown. It is a scattered landscape of low buildings, parking lots, signs, and enticing advertising images deferring to the car. Las Vegas did not invent these suburban forms. They are typical of all commercial strips. Las Vegas' contribution lies in exaggerating and intensifying the features of a strip. Fed by enormous gambling revenues, budgets for Strip hotels were larger than most other strip districts could dream of. The Strip also concentrated single-mindedly on recreation, avoiding the grimy repair shops and mundane shopping centers found on other strips. Over the years Las Vegas has helped to mature the ordinary vocabulary of the commercial strip into a vivid urban center with public landmarks, public spaces, and public purposes.

Many noted architects grappled with the design of a city which would accommodate the car. Most failed. Edgar Chambless' Roadtown of 1910 proposed a ribbon building containing houses, stores, and subways that snaked through the countryside. Le Corbusier campaigned for multistory viaduct highways running on the roofs of apartments in São Paulo, Brazil, in 1929, in Algiers in 1930, and in Rio de Janeiro in 1936. Frank Lloyd Wright came closest to a buildable plan with his 1934 Broadacre City proposal which swore off high-density concentration in favor of sprawl. Such schemes have turned out to be only sideshows in the course of urban growth. To find real, functioning (if flawed) car-oriented districts, we have to look to Las Vegas' Strip and other strips of the commercial roadside. Henry Ford's mammoth,

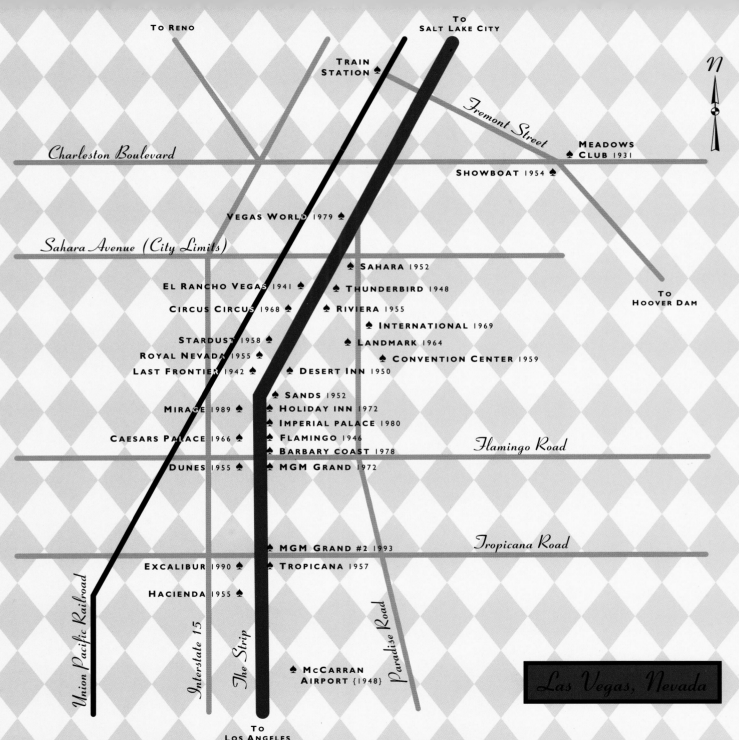

TO RENO

TO
SALT LAKE CITY

TRAIN
STATION ♠

Fremont Street

MEADOWS
CLUB 1931 ♠

Charleston Boulevard

SHOWBOAT 1954 ♠

VEGAS WORLD 1979 ♠

Sahara Avenue (City Limits)

♠ SAHARA 1952

EL RANCHO VEGAS 1941 ♠   ♠ THUNDERBIRD 1948

CIRCUS CIRCUS 1968 ♠   ♠ RIVIERA 1955

♠ INTERNATIONAL 1969

STARDUST 1958 ♠   ♠ LANDMARK 1964

ROYAL NEVADA 1955 ♠   ♠ CONVENTION CENTER 1959

LAST FRONTIER 1942 ♠   ♠ DESERT INN 1950

♠ SANDS 1952

MIRAGE 1989 ♠   ♠ HOLIDAY INN 1972

♠ IMPERIAL PALACE 1980

CAESARS PALACE 1966 ♠   ♠ FLAMINGO 1946

♠ BARBARY COAST 1978

Flamingo Road

DUNES 1955 ♠   ♠ MGM GRAND 1972

TO
HOOVER DAM

♠ MGM GRAND #2 1993

Tropicana Road

EXCALIBUR 1990 ♠   ♠ TROPICANA 1957

HACIENDA 1955 ♠

Union Pacific Railroad

Interstate 15

The Strip

Paradise Road

♠ McCARRAN
AIRPORT {1948}

Las Vegas, Nevada

TO
LOS ANGELES

muscular River Rouge factory in Dearborn, Michigan, of 1917 was celebrated as the ultimate creation of mass-scale production. For the latter half of the century, Las Vegas is a parallel car culture artifact for mass-scale recreation.

Yet it is Las Vegas that has been treated as the sideshow by most established urbanists and critics. After all, it's only a carnival city off in the desert, many critics and architects reasoned. Lewis Mumford found any generic strip in 1962 "an incoherent and purposeless urbanoid nonentity." Las Vegas "looks like a grotesque Disneyland," wrote journalists Ed Reid and Ovid Demaris in 1963. The garish dazzle of neon and the astounding array of styles have made Las Vegas an easy target for lampoon.

It may be just as well that most professional planners left strips alone as they grew. Freed from the strictures of architectural theory and high-art taste, strips could often respond to the economic energy, commercial forces, and cultural inspiration at play in midcentury America. Rather than developing methodically, Las Vegas' Strip grew by experiment, mistakes, wild visions, pragmatic solutions, and chaotic collage. It became "collective art," Reyner Banham asserted, as thousands of independent decisions by clients, architects, sign artists, governmental officials, and marketing mystics (divining the taste of the people) accumulated over decades into the Las Vegas of today. This is the essence of commercial vernacular architecture, the everyday architecture responding to popular and economic demands in fast-food restaurants, housing tracts, malls, gas stations, cineplexes, and all the mundane buildings that constitute most of the buildings in our cities. For fifty years Las Vegas has been an outdoor museum of American popular culture.

The results were by no means always successful. Las Vegas has succeeded no better than most urbanizing suburbs in controlling traffic congestion or channeling growth wisely. Like many other cities, it faces problems of scarce water and economic stratification. But this strapping experimental prototype community of tomorrow has found innovative forms for the traditional cultural infrastructure of a city, the orienting landmarks, the public arenas that mix pedestrians with cars, the messages and media of cultural communication. For many other evolving strips, it has lessons.

Is there a Las Vegas style? If so it has always been changing. Popularly, Las Vegas is identified with glitz, neon, vulgarity, and excess. Like neon, the city is by turns crassly commercial and sublimely beautiful. But how did Las Vegas grow? Where did these forms come from? Does the city have roots? Does it have a history? This books attempts to answer these questions.

Las Vegas has had six architectural eras so far. First, there was the protostrip of the 1930s, an incubation period when a few gas stations and billboards lined a ribbon of asphalt. Except for a few casinos, downtown's Fremont Street was indistinguishable from the standard Midwest Main Street.

The second period, the birth of the Strip, began in 1939, when the first casinos appeared, followed closely by the first motor hotel, El Rancho Vegas, designed as a luxurious dude ranch. Fremont Street boomed during World War II as defense workers flocked to Las Vegas.

The third era commenced in 1946 with a string of glorified

motels (beginning with the Flamingo) in a sumptuous and sophisticated modern style. Las Vegas met the national boom in tourism with an aggressive promotion campaign.

The fourth period began in 1958 with the Stardust. By turning its sign into its architecture, the Stardust established an unconventional but effective response to the Strip site. It had learned a lesson from the Fremont Street signs, which were already growing in scale. In turn, downtown's Golden Nugget and Horseshoe Club learned from the Stardust by creating entire facades of neon.

The opening of Caesars Palace in 1966 marked a fifth era, the era of the theme, where each Strip resort created its own mini-world based on history, fantasy, or exotic locales.

Around 1980 Las Vegas entered the current and sixth era influenced by large hotel corporations. The skyline once dominated by highrise signs was now walled in with highrise towers. The sparse recreational strip became a dense urban corridor.

The evolution of Las Vegas isn't easy to trace. America's tendency to brush the historical tracks from the trail applies in spades to Las Vegas. It is only by chance that a few fragments of the original casinos survive today. Little attempt has been made to document them. Many astute observers have been misled by the Strip's ever-changing shell game. Even Tom Wolfe's seminal 1964 essay in *Esquire*, "Las Vegas (What?) Las Vegas (Can't Hear You! Too Noisy!) Las Vegas!!!!," identified the Flamingo Hotel's cylindrical sign ("covered from top to bottom with neon rings in the shape of bubbles that fizzed all eight stories up into the desert sky all night long like an illuminated whisky-

soda tumbler filled to the brim with pink champagne") as part of gangster Benjamin "Bugsy" Siegel's original hotel. In fact, it was part of a remodel in 1953, six years after Siegel's assassination. The nature of Siegel's seminal vision (less splashy, less neon, more Californian) is blurred by the lack of accurate documentation.

To his great credit, Wolfe did interview several of the actual sign artists working in Las Vegas in 1964. Most critics have treated Las Vegas' architecture as a natural curiosity without author. But as Reyner Banham noted in 1970, "Anyone who views Vegas as if it were a work of nature like the Grand Canyon or the Aurora Borealis is going to miss the cream of it. Visually, it is the triumph of human skill over great odds, all probability and moral law."

To put that skill on the record is one intent of this book. It documents the evolution of the major Strip hotels, their signs, highrise towers, casinos, pools, showrooms, and parking lots. The Strip was not born full-blown from the brow of Ben Siegel. It has changed over the years. Overwhelmed by the light and color, visitors today are likely to see Las Vegas as a unified tapestry. In fact it is a collage of many different eras and styles. For example, the shimmering highrise signs of the Dunes, the Stardust, and the Frontier, now inextricably linked in the public eye with Las Vegas, were all built in the space of four short years in the mid-1960s. Woven into today's riveting panorama of castles and volcanoes, they become detached from their own history.

Other icons of the city have disappeared. The demolition of the classic Golden Nugget and Mint facades in the late 1980s, major losses for historic preservation, passed with hardly a whisper of protest. If

they have disappeared from the street, it is this book's intent that they will not disappear from architectural history.

Delving into Las Vegas' history has turned out to be an archaeological dig through the recent past. With revolving doors in the owners' suites of every hotel on the Strip, drawings and photographs have often been lost over the years. Some dates proved elusive; I have attempted to provide a close approximation whenever the exact date could not be verified. Indispensable to this dig have been the resources of commercial photographers, particularly the Las Vegas News Bureau and the Manis Collection at the University of Nevada, Las Vegas, Special Collections. Their purpose was publicity, not history, but so thoroughly did they photograph Las Vegas that they have provided a rich resource for tracking the development of the Las Vegas style.

Unfortunately, the available material has rarely been tapped, despite the tremendous significance of Las Vegas as an American icon. We know much more about Elvis Presley's birth than we do about the Strip's. The most thorough and insightful analysis of the Strip is, of course, *Learning from Las Vegas* by Robert Venturi, Denise Scott Brown, and Steven Izenour. The product of a Yale School of Art and Architecture studio which took students to Las Vegas in 1968, the book was published in 1972. Before that book, one must backtrack twenty years to find another serious, thorough look at commercial strips. J. B. Jackson's series of articles in *Landscape* magazine in the early 1950s challenged architects and planners to look at strips freshly as vital, new urban expressions that needed to be understood, not ignored. *Learning from Las Vegas* drew the subject to the surface of the profession's consciousness, but it led to few

further studies, references to Las Vegas examples in the academic literature, or documentation of the city's changes in the last twenty years. This book records some of those changes.

The architectural rules of the road for strip cities are different from those for traditional cities. It is today even more pressing to understand the strengths and weaknesses, the history and trends in the strip form. Las Vegas provides one useful case study.

I am an admirer of the commercial vernacular. It can achieve a directness (even through layers of glitz) which can be pragmatic or imaginative. It is accessible to a wide audience. If much commercial vernacular architecture is prosaic, so is much highly publicized high-art architecture. But when the commercial vernacular hits the mark, it can compare in freshness, insight and appropriateness with the best architecture anywhere. Las Vegas is not an ideal city. But it is well worth the study.

♠　♦　♣　♥

A WORD ON WORDS: *Strip* when capitalized, refers to the Las Vegas Strip; *strip* refers to the generic urban form. I often use Las Vegas as a general term to refer to the architectural phenomena of the Strip and Fremont Street collectively, although this is technically inaccurate as the Strip is outside the city limits of Las Vegas. What we call the Strip has had several names over the years, including the Arrowhead Highway, the Los Angeles Highway, Route 91, and Las Vegas Boulevard South.

I have limited the focus of this book to an architectural history

of the two neighborhoods influenced by gambling and recreation, the Strip and Fremont Street. The bibliography lists books that focus on other facets of the city: its general history and planning, the history of crime and gambling, social history, and architectural theory. I recommend these for a fuller understanding of the city. I have also limited my discussion of several intriguing tangents. Worth further exploration is the relationship between entertainment styles and Las Vegas, including the practical questions of stagecraft and theater configurations, and the cultural ties between Sophie Tucker and the Last Frontier, Noel Coward and the Desert Inn, Liberace and the Riviera, Louis Prima and the Sahara, Bob Wills and the Golden Nugget, Frank Sinatra and the Sands, and, of course, Elvis Presley and the Hilton. The relation of Las Vegas to Reno, Atlantic City, and resort architecture elsewhere requires attention. Las Vegas' changing ecology, the impact of air-conditioning, and the role of security will be fruitful topics for others. I have also, reluctantly, not dealt with the wedding chapels of Las Vegas. There is a lot more to learn from Las Vegas.

♠ ♦ ♣ ♥

I THANK THOSE architects, engineers, and designers who were personally involved with the design of Las Vegas, and who agreed to be interviewed: Wayne McAllister, Martin Stern, Jr., Harris Sharp, Tom Turner, T. Y. Lin, Hugh Taylor, Kermit Wayne, Milton Schwartz, Brian Webb, Veldon Simpson, Lee Linton, Charles Barnard, Joel Bergman, and Harold Bradford and Rudy Crisostomo of Young Electric Sign Company.

Dozens of people have helped me in researching and preparing the ideas in this book. I thank Dennis McBride and the Special Collections of the University of Nevada, Las Vegas; Donn Knepp and the Las Vegas News Bureau; Frank Wright and David Milman of the Nevada State Historical Society; Michael Griffin and the Del Webb Corporation; John Janulaw of the Luckman Partnership; and Luigi Mumford and the Art Institute of Chicago. I also thank Eugene Moehring, Patrick Gaffey, George Tate, Robert Stoldal, Robert Hess, Colin Russell, Robert Ehrlich, Al Balboni, Dale Furman, Keith Stone, Lee Hamovitz, John English, Paul Fees, and many others. Special thanks and gratitude go to Jim Heimann, Robert Bruegmann, Steven Izenour, David Gebhard, John Chase, Margaret Crawford, John Pastier, and Barbara and Charles Hess. My gratitude goes to my family, Tiena, Nash, and Zoe Hess, for their sterling patience while I was writing this book. In addition, I thank those who have contributed to my awareness and delight in architecture and this subject through their writings: J. B. Jackson, Robert Venturi, Denise Scott Brown, Reyner Banham, and, particularly, noted authority John Beach. John, I wish you could have read this.

In America, illusion and reality are still often the same thing.
The dream is the achievement, the achievement is the dream.

GAVIN LAMBERT, **THE SLIDE AREA**, 1959

Cowboys 'n' Cadillacs: 1855—1940

THE STORY OF Las Vegas is the story of the unexpected twists of the American road. At first the roads were footpaths, then wagon roads, then railroads, then highways. All brought people ready to be astonished at what they found on the road.

If the road gave Las Vegas form, then the West gave it substance. The western site freed Las Vegas from the distractions and inhibitions of the East; the desert's blank slate permitted towns to grow according to the winds of culture and the dictates of commerce. Tollhouses, livery stables, train stations, roadhouses, taverns, motels, and gas stations lining the road began by serving travelers on their way to someplace else. But slowly the path became a destination itself. That's how frontiers turn nowhere into somewhere.

Entrepreneurs soon discovered that western imagery and atmosphere could be mined as profitably as silver and gold. The working West of ranching and mining and the urban West of commerce and trade grew up alongside the legendary West of dime novels and Buffalo Bill Cody's Wild West Show. The historical architecture of tepees, hogans, and adobe pueblos was joined by the agrarian vernacular of Spanish haciendas and missions, the industrial vernacular of mines, bunkhouses, and ranch houses, and the urban commercial vernacular of saloons and false-front towns that culminated in the barbaric opulence of Victorian San Francisco, Denver, and Fort Worth. Each style provided a distinct and marketable image in the East.

Prime purveyors of this imagery were the western railroads.

They stood to gain customers by advertising the wonders of the West in the East, but they also felt the need to be sure tourists got their money's worth once they arrived. To this end, the Fred Harvey Company, formed in 1876, built a series of self-consciously westernized railroad stations, hotels, restaurants, and gift shops for the Atchison, Topeka & Santa Fe Railroad to amplify the "westernness" of the western road.

Las Vegas was a roadtown long before its official founding in 1905. First known by Europeans as a place along a wagon trail where a creek and meadows (*vegas* in Spanish) lay, the site was later visited by Col. John C. Frémont, Kit Carson, and other explorers who would leave their names on streets, casinos, and motels. When Congress established a mail route from Salt Lake City to San Diego in April 1854, it also designated $25,000 to build a military road to protect the route, which passed through the Las Vegas valley. A year later, Mormon settlers traveled down the road from Salt Lake City to found a fort at the site. That first gamble to make the place profitable agriculturally and to convert the native Paiutes failed due to internal dissension among the Mormons and an Indian raid in 1858. The Mormons turned back up the road.

The mail road was upgraded to the Los Angeles/Salt Lake wagon road in 1865 and thrived

♣

FREMONT AND FIRST STREETS, C. 1908. BEFORE IT BECAME FILLED WITH THEMED WESTERN ARCHITECTURE, LAS VEGAS WAS AN ACTUAL WESTERN TOWN WITH A SPANISH-STYLE TRAIN STATION AND FALSE-FRONT FACADES FRONTING PLANK SIDEWALKS.

as an artery that provided supplies and transportation to the Comstock mine and other regional lodes. In 1902 the vast western geometry came to Las Vegas' aid. The undistinguished meadow became the center point between Los Angeles and Salt Lake City when Montana Senator William Clark's San Pedro, Los Angeles & Salt Lake Railroad (later merged into the Union Pacific) needed a locale for water, repair shops, and icehouses to service its trains. Las Vegas was the logical choice. The wagon road was updated into a railroad.

The first successful town on the site was a roadtown—a railroad town. The railroad governed the town's design, shifting it twenty-seven degrees off north to accommodate the straightest run for track through the flat valley. Las Vegas was a prototypical railroad town: a gridiron of blocks paralleling the tracks. In theory, a grid can be stretched in all directions infinitely and equally. It is the perfect form, in the eyes of civic boosters, for a town with no limit to its potential. The railroad station weighted this grid at one point. Within the vast space of the desert, the railroad decided to stop the train at one place, which became the town's gateway. At this portal, at the head of Fremont Street, people stepped off the train. The most valuable lots sold at the 1905 real estate auction were therefore those nearest the station. All other districts fanned out from this point in decreasing value.

A tent town sprung up in time for the auction. The town's first hotel, opening with thirty rooms the day before the land auction, had a canvas roof. The most solid building in town was the train station, but even it had an air of impermanence as it was a train car. A more solid town of brick and board soon leaped into existence with a handful of buildings displaying the vernacular false fronts of frontier towns. By 1908 the corner of First and Fremont already had a crenellated castle with an octagonal tower, and a Greek temple bank. Signs in 1908 were thin, wooden, and horizontal, and announced services: baths, shoe shop, groceries, drugstore. A western economy permeated the town in the early years; ranching, cattle, and horses remained a major part of Nevada culture well into the 1930s. Though artesian wells were discovered, the valley never became a large agricultural area.

Not long after 1905, the grandest building by far was the railroad station. This Mission Revival structure was a modest version of the sumptuous haciendas, pueblos, and missions that the Fred Harvey Company built and managed as railroad hotels and restaurants along the western train lines. The 1902 Alvarado Hotel by architect Charles Whittlesey in Albuquerque provided a stylistic template, a Spanish Mission building with a determined use of Native American artifacts and patterns in decoration. In the Las Vegas station, heavily textured stucco walls rose into a looping silhouette; arcades ran around the outside as protection from the summer sun. The location established the dominance and wealth of the east side of town for most of the century. The eastern orientation doomed a slightly earlier rival town site on the west side of the tracks due to the initial difficulty wagons had getting over the tracks.

Wood roofs sheltered boardwalks along the dirt street; some roofs were lined with balustrades in a style familiar to later generations of western movie fans. Gambling and liquor sales were limited to a red-light district in Block 16, north of First Street between Ogden and Stewart avenues.

Although Las Vegas was founded in the twentieth century, its architecture, materials, and plan could have been seen in Arizona, Kansas, or Colorado twenty or thirty years before, at the height of the western expansion. Simplicity of construction and a dearth of materials dictated the city's design. Some mining towns of the period were much more elaborate. Nearby Rhyolite, also founded in 1905, boasted a grand three-story stone bank.

The first stretch of Fremont was paved in 1909. The same year, Clark County was created, a critical development for the future Strip. Everything outside city limits was under looser governmental controls, a benign atmosphere in which the future hotel casinos could take root and thrive along the county highway. In spite of repeated efforts by the city of Las Vegas to annex this area after the Strip burgeoned, this border zone with lenient zoning and lower taxes remained inviolable.

By 1925 Fremont Street was paved all the way to Fifth Street, and Fifth was paved all the way south to the town line. South of there Fifth became the Los Angeles Highway. Pavement heralded the future, and it did not belong to the railroad or the railroad town. It belonged to the automobile. By democratizing tourism, the automobile took more people to more distant places than ever before. The highway was the latest version of the wagon roads and railroad lines that brought people west in the first place.

In much of the West, a new tourist architecture began to be built in the 1920s. Most of the first western tourists were rugged adventurers who camped out. For the wealthier, the road was still rugged, but Fred Harvey offered guided trips, the Indian Detours, where caravans of sixteen-cylinder Packard and Cadillac touring cars, driven by costumed drivers, took tourists into Indian country to pueblos and other sights inaccessible by train. At night they returned to the comforts of La Fonda in Santa Fe, New Mexico, a puebloid hotel from 1920 by architects T. H. Rapp, W. M. Rapp, and A. C. Henrickson. So successful were the Indian Detours that La Fonda had to be tripled in size in 1926 by architects John Gaw Meem and Mary Colter. The additions showed a rapid increase in sophistication and knowledge in the ways to use and apply historical western models.

A two-hour car drive for Angelenos, Palm Springs, California, also began developing as a resort in the mid-1920s. Its glamour became the envy of many Las Vegans, who wanted their city to be a desert playground for the rich and famous. Partly in response, Las Vegas opened its first golf course in 1927. Palm Springs remained small, dotted with self-contained spas. The rambling Desert Inn had a tile roof and wood beam ceilings echoing the Mission Revival, with terraces, palms, and gardens. More adventurous architecturally was the 1923 Oasis Hotel by architect Lloyd Wright, who had learned architecture in the office of his famous father Frank. Over the years Palm Springs attracted many noted architects who kept its style understated.

Tucson and Phoenix, Arizona, likewise developed tourist economies. The 1927 Arizona Biltmore in Phoenix by Frank Lloyd Wright used western themes expressed with native materials and craggy surfaces. Though distinctively Wrightian, it borrowed motifs and massing from Mayan architecture in a clear evocation of the region's prehistory.

But these large resorts were not the only new tourist architecture. A new roadside vernacular architecture grew out of tourist cabins and courts: the motel.

After the number of passengers riding the Atchison, Topeka & Santa Fe Railroad through the West peaked in 1920, the car began to compete more intensely with the railroad. Cars dictated less expensive, less formal, more dispersed lodgings for noncamping travelers. Although motels were a national phenomenon, they were well suited to take over from Harvey Houses as fixtures on the western tourist landscape. Many motels celebrated the exotic experience of the West, as had Harvey Houses. Travelers stopping anywhere from Kansas to California might sleep or dine in a tepee; the aura of pueblos and ranches was popular.

The archetypal western motel of the 1930s and early 1940s stood on a spacious piece of property on the road into town, and in smaller towns often backed up onto desert or fields. These motor courts were arranged on their lots for the convenience of cars: plenty of room to turn in, a parking space or attached garage conveniently close to each room. A registration office stood by the entry, often the owner's house adapted to the purpose. In the 1920s the individual cabins of the motor court were set out in a U shape with the open end pointed to the road. By the 1930s the cabins were often linked together for economy into a unified U- or L-shaped wing. They were set back, away from the highway noise. Lawn often surrounded the buildings. The layout guaranteed a certain spaciousness; after all, land was cheap on the protostrip.

The ubiquitous feature of all motels was the identifying roadside sign, often neon, often with a picture depicting the theme of the restaurant or an attraction in the area. Messages on the sign called attention to the motel's features: pool and air-conditioning in the fancier ones, cleanliness, a Duncan Hines approval rating, a coffee shop. A pool was a great attraction and was often featured at the front of the motel right on the highway as a visible lure to weary travelers seeking refreshment. If not located up front, the pool was set back and surrounded on three or four sides by the room wings, especially in motels that aspired to resort status.

To appeal to roadside customers, motel builders often called on the evocative symbols of an earlier West. While some motels were literally as utilitarian as bunkhouses, many others adopted their imagery, mating a traditional image with a distinctly modern type. Walls of adobelike blocks with weeping mortar formalized the irregularities of Native American adobes. Roofs were shake or mission tile, and covers

FREMONT AND FIRST STREETS, C. 1929. BEFORE GAMBLING WAS LEGALIZED, LAS VEGAS CELEBRATED THE FEDERAL GOVERNMENT'S DECISION TO BUILD HOOVER DAM NEARBY.

along the walkways in front of the rooms approximated a ranch-house porch with heavy wood beams and posts. Motels may have been a new, functional building type, but historic symbolism was often critical to their success. In the 1880s, as fascination with the West grew, the vernacular fabricated bunkhouse clothes hooks out of deer antlers were expanded into steer-horn rocking chairs and hat racks made for easterners by furniture designers. In the same spirit, lariats, broncos, Mexicans, sunsets, cowboy hats, pueblos, sombreros, Indian heads, wagons, war bonnets, cactus, and cow skulls appeared in such diverse motel fixtures as tin signs, interior furnishings, and coffee shop placemats. Similarly the coffee shop of Hertzka and Knowles' 1940 Paso Robles Inn in California was ornamented with a mural of early ranch life. The images connoted wide open spaces, broad clear skies, and freedom from care. The rustic western motifs often contrasted with the touches of luxury increasingly demanded by tourists.

The rapid growth of this commercial roadside landscape attracted little attention in the professional press. It was not generally considered architecture. "On the approaches to cities such as Denver and Los Angeles [motels] form what is almost a roadslum," wrote one of the few critics to contemplate the change, Douglas Haskell, in *Architectural*

Record in 1937. "When all this has been said there remains in their favor that they are growing with the people themselves and represent healthy new ways of living, at least on vacation. There has been much talk about an architecture of 'light and air'; this puts it into action. It is not elegant but appeals to the mass of the people and grows out of their desires . . . the camps are branching into a variety of embryonic communities."

Cities nationwide had developed strips decades before. At first they were one- or two-story commercial buildings lining the trolley tracks linking the traditional downtown to new suburbs. After World War I, the automobile caused strips to be spread even farther out into the changing countryside. Los Angeles was especially well suited to this pattern of urban growth: Venice Boulevard was oriented to the interurban tracks running down its center, with low commercial buildings (contrasting with the taller blocks of the downtown core) lining the sidewalk for easy access. Wilshire Boulevard's Miracle Mile, "the true ancestor of the western Strip . . . a linear stretched-out automotive downtown, the kind of townmaking that is natural and native to the motor age," as Reyner Banham called it, was a fashionable strip challenging the traditional downtown in the late 1920s. Its buildings fronted on the sidewalk, but large parking lots at the rear accommodated customers arriving by auto. Sunset Strip, a recreational strip developed in the mid-1920s beyond the Los Angeles city limits between Hollywood and Beverly Hills, attracted legally marginal operations. From its earliest days, gambling was known at clubs like La Boheme. Zoning and law enforcement were usually more lenient on strips, especially if they lay under looser county jurisdiction. North of Sunset, the San Fernando Valley's Ventura Boulevard was still a semirural route in the 1930s studded with a few small towns, motels, gas stations, and drive-ins.

The roadside motel might seem an unlikely cornerstone for any city; yet the motel was the basic building block of today's Strip. It determined the siting of rooms, casinos, pools, and other recreation, and dictated the importance of signage. Whereas San Francisco was based on the row house set on a twenty-five-foot lot, the Las Vegas Strip was based on the motel set on a thousand-foot frontage. The motel model's strong reliance on imagery to convey a sense of place was a stunningly effective method of place making. Those images sometimes seemed unlikely. Tepees were transformed into motels, and Indian chiefs into neon signs. But such deadpan transfiguration was not uncommon, at least in the West. Wright turned Mayan temples into the sybaritic Arizona Biltmore; the Watchtower, designed in 1934 by Harvey architect Mary Colter on the edge of the Grand Canyon, re-created a sacred Indian kiva, remodeled with panoramic picture windows of nature's wonders. Las Vegas would more than encourage this sort of transformation.

But Las Vegas was not considered a tourist destination in the early 1930s. Las Vegas' own landscape was not so dramatic as that of Palm Springs or Phoenix; the Paiutes had not left anything so picturesque as the New Mexico pueblos. But then the United States government stepped in to provide Las Vegas with its touristic raison d'être.

Amid the desert, hundreds of miles from anything that could be called a city, the federal government chose to flex its muscles and imagination in the Great Depression by building an engineering marvel. Damming the Colorado River, it created Lake Mead, whose water and hydroelectric power would nourish the growth of cities and agriculture throughout the West. Hoover Dam was to be as extravagant a declaration of the human presence in the wilderness as Las Vegas itself would eventually become. Both were artificial constructs in the natural desert. The dam would be mighty, awesome, beneficent, and perhaps ultimately terrible in the urban sprawl it nurtured. The city would be opulent, flimsy, and indelible.

The building of Hoover Dam barely thirty miles from Las Vegas, approved in 1928, would mean a boost to the local economy at the start of the Great Depression. President Herbert Hoover's Department of the Interior had rejected Las Vegas as headquarters for dam construction even before gambling was legalized, declaring it "a boisterous frontier town," and instead built an entire planned community near the dam site for worker housing. The community, Boulder City, became a model for good planning and was managed strictly; it opted not to allow gambling. Yet workers still traveled to Las Vegas to spend their money after working hours. In March of 1931, the same year excavation for the dam began, the Nevada legislature legalized gambling. Also in 1931, it made divorces easier by lowering residency requirements to six weeks.

The influx of workers produced a boom in Las Vegas. Even after the legalization of statewide gambling, the self-anointed City of Destiny was slow to realize the potential market for gambling. It was outstripped by Nevada's largest city, Reno, where Raymond Smith's Harolds Club began to turn back-room gambling into public entertainment. The first legal gambling clubs in Las Vegas were simply business as usual. Gambling, which had been legal at statehood in 1864, was prohibited in 1909 but continued to be tolerated in the back rooms of clubs and bars. Far from imagining a future Monte Carlo in the desert, the Nevada legislature simply wanted to control the underground gambling already in existence and to tap its revenue. Locals were the main market; no larger vision sparked the approval of gambling. The first gambling license in Clark County went to Mayme Stocker of the Northern Club, a Fremont Street bar and restaurant which had opened in the mid-1920s. Five other licenses granted in 1931 in Las Vegas went to clubs on Fremont Street between First and Third (later extended to Fifth), near the old red-light district.

Through most of the 1930s, gambling remained a sidelight for Las Vegas, a steady but minor industry consisting of the clubs along

♥

FREMONT AND SECOND STREETS, C. 1933. RENO, NOT LAS VEGAS, BECAME NEVADA'S FIRST GAMBLING CENTER. BESIDES THE NEW HOTEL APACHE AND THE BOULDER CLUB NEXT DOOR, LITTLE CHANGED ON FREMONT STREET IN THE 1930S.

MEADOWS

♦

MEADOWS CLUB, BOULDER HIGHWAY, 1931, PAUL WARNER. FIFTEEN YEARS BEFORE THE FLAMINGO OPENED, GLAMOROUS GAMBLING HAD ALREADY ARRIVED ON A HIGHWAY ON THE OUTSKIRTS OF LAS VEGAS. "ELEGANT IN ITS SUAVE APPOINTMENTS," AS THE LOCAL PAPER REPORTED, THE SPANISH COLONIAL REVIVAL MEADOWS WAS THE FIRST SOPHISTICATED CASINO/NIGHTCLUB AND HOTEL TO EXPLOIT NEVADA'S LEGAL GAMBLING. THE CABARET FILLED THE LEFT WING; THE CASINO WAS BEHIND THE ARCHES ON THE RIGHT.

Fremont Street. Featuring bars, poker tables, and slot machines, the clubs were largely a domain of serious male card players. But the eighth wonder of the world, as Boulder Dam (renamed during Democrat Franklin Roosevelt's presidency) was billed, began to funnel a torrent of tourists through town to monitor construction and admire the results. Some Las Vegas leaders envisioned their region as a tourist attraction and their town as its center. With visions of a Nevada Palm Springs dancing in their heads, they began to promote their characteristic western identity—the desert scenery, a social mix of laissez-faire government and neighborly hospitality embodied in the speedy divorces and easy gambling the state made available—and a massive reclamation project. The state's federal right to legislate gambling, says historian Daniel Boorstin, made "a new resource out of statehood itself." Legislation was the state's main commodity.

Outsiders from Los Angeles would discover and exploit the potential at the Meadows Club. A brief description makes the Meadows seem prescient: a combination casino, hotel, dinner club, and nightclub located outside the city

limits on a main highway. It was owned by a Los Angeles underworld figure. But this was fifteen years before Bugsy Siegel opened his landmark Flamingo. This owner was Tony Cornero.

Antonio Cornero Stralla, known as Tony Cornero, and his brothers Frank and Louis received one of the first Clark County gambling licenses and opened the Meadows Club May 2, 1931, on the Boulder Highway near Twenty-fifth Street just outside city limits. Cornero, a bootlegger to the Los Angeles carriage trade in the 1920s, had been caught and given two years in federal prison in 1926. He escaped and went underground only to surrender himself late in 1929. He served his term until 1930, just prior to the Meadows' opening. His brothers Louis and Frank officially fronted the operation.

Although a supper club with entertainment was unusual in Las Vegas, similar gambling clubs existed in Los Angeles in the 1930s. The Mission-style building was designed and built by local architect Paul Warner. "Entering through the main doors, the visitor finds himself in a long wide foyer, arched entrances on the left opening into the cabaret or ball room and on the right into the gaming hall. . . . The [gaming] room is large and well ventilated and a cushion-tile flooring will soften the steps of those who gather here," wrote the *Las Vegas Age* on May 2, 1931.

It was hardly a sawdust joint. "All metallic design is in pure gold and silver leaf," reported the *Age*. "One who has visited other Casinos could easily imagine a glimpse from the window would reveal the softly lapping waters of a dark blue Mediterranean under a Latin moon." In later years Las Vegas would offer a new casino paradigm, but for now the aristocratic European model still held the public's imagination.

The Meadows also had fifty hotel rooms operated under lease to Alex Richmond, owner of several California hotels including the Arlington in Santa Barbara. The nightclub was plush; diners wore coats and ties. Car-oriented, the Meadows was well sited to attract Boulder Dam workers heading into town with their paychecks. The Corneros hoped to bring in Southern Californians on a nearby airstrip. Other, less distinguished casinos such as the Black Cat and the Red Windmill (which featured a windmill) also stood along the Boulder Highway. But the Meadows attracted no major imitators. The Corneros transferred the casino operation to associates in 1932. It lasted until 1936, the same year the dam project was completed and Boulder Dam began generating electricity. But Las Vegas had not seen the last of Tony Cornero.

One reason Cornero's Los Angeles colleagues didn't expand into Las Vegas when gambling was legalized in 1931 was that gamblers did not need to travel seven or eight hours through the desert. Southern Californians who wanted to gamble legally were able to drive four hours south to Tijuana, Mexico, where architect Wayne McAllister had designed the luxurious Agua Caliente resort, opened in 1926. It included a casino and track close enough to the Los Angeles market to make commercial sense. When the Agua Caliente closed in 1935 after President Lázaro Cárdenas outlawed gambling in Mexico, Los Angeles gamblers were not inconvenienced too much; a year earlier horse racing had begun at Santa Anita racetrack, close to Los Angeles and an easier drive than Tijuana.

Since 1928, gambling could be enjoyed off Santa Monica pier on several gambling boats, including Tony Cornero's SS *Rex*, an old collier stripped of engines and anchored three miles offshore in 1938, outside California jurisdiction. Gamblers could go to the Clover and Colony clubs in Culver City or to clubs along the Sunset Strip, relatively open gambling houses and nightclubs that were chic, elegant, and blessed with a cachet by the Hollywood stars who frequented them. The Sunset Strip, in county not city jurisdiction, thrived. The city of Los Angeles turned a blind eye on gambling within its limits. Bribery helped, and the administration of Mayor Frank Shaw became infamous

as one of the most corrupt in Los Angeles history.

In spite of Las Vegas' slow start, the foundations of the incipient neon city were laid on Fremont Street in the 1930s. Between 1930 and 1932, many of the one-story wood shacks were replaced by prosperous two-story brick structures. The two-story reinforced concrete Nevada Hotel (later the Sal Sagev, since 1955 the Golden Gate) across from the train station added a third floor in 1931. Drugstores, banks, bakeries, and other businesses stood beside the relative handful of casinos. Small storefronts dominated the street. State Cafe, Ethel's Liquor Store, shoe shops, and other establishments had standard signs of the period. While the storefronts had typical display windows, the casinos had frontages lined with wood and swinging glass doors to make entrance easy. These were replaced in the late 1930s with sliding glass panels, which opened the clubs to the sidewalk. Off Fremont, laundries, icehouses, and other service buildings tapered off into the scrubland.

Fremont Street's architectural design was eclectic. The basic buildings were a mix of one- and two-story commercial fronts; several were variations of stucco Mission and brick Victorian styles with a bit of appropriate Classicism used in bank buildings. Despite a few overtly western touches (the Las Vegas bar had a neon Indian head sign), Fremont

FREMONT STREET FROM UNION PACIFIC STATION, C. 1938.
THE MAIN CASINOS ALL HAD PROMINENT NEON SIGNS, BUT SO DID THE OVERLAND AND SAL SAGEV HOTELS.

Street was not self-consciously western in style. A few buildings remained from the beginning of the century, when Las Vegas was an authentic western town, but most of the architecture was similar to that found along contemporary main streets nationwide. The 1929 Boulder Club (described by Paul Ralli as "a working man's hangout") and the Las Vegas Club (opened in the mid-1920s, formerly the Smokeshop) streamlined their facades into modest versions of the Moderne using plate glass windows, chrome trim, and black Vitrolite. The glint of chrome emphasized the appealingly modern air-conditioning inside, a technological advance that would make a resort Las Vegas possible.

♠

PAIR-O-DICE CLUB, c. 1938.
A FEW CASINOS CATERING TO THE CAR TRADE LINED THE LOS ANGELES HIGHWAY OUTSIDE CITY LIMITS EVEN BEFORE HOTELS ARRIVED. SPANISH IN STYLE LIKE THE MEADOWS CLUB, THE PAIR-O-DICE LATER BECAME 91 CLUB AND IN 1942 WAS INCORPORATED INTO THE LAST FRONTIER HOTEL.

The gem of the new downtown was the three-story Hotel Apache, designed by local architect A. Lacy Worswick. It opened in March 1932, a year after the legalization of gambling. The hundred-room hotel was as sophisticated as the town could imagine. An elevator rose to a supper club on the top floor. Canvas awnings sheltered the store windows of a cafe, drugstore, and lobby on the hotel's ground floor. Inside, zigzag corners decorated the interior arches, a motif borrowed from Native American designs and used to convey a western tone. In the mid-1930s the ground-floor Apache Bar was the plushest casino in town, with its own neon sign and terra-cotta facing.

Neon, the medium that was to make Las

Vegas famous, was already present on Fremont Street, but its application was hardly exceptional. Arriving in the United States in 1923 from France, neon was first used commercially for the Earl C. Anthony Packard dealership in Los Angeles. The 1933 Chicago World's Fair, produced extravaganzas of neon lighting which the Depression-clad country could admire but could rarely afford to copy. Nevertheless commercial signs soon developed a neon vernacular of outlined letters and floral or zigzag Moderne ornament. Soon it was effectively and elegantly integrated into architecture, as in architect Wayne McAllister's series of Los Angeles drive-in restaurants. It reached into interiors as well, as neon curtains hanging from the patent leather ceiling of Hollywood's 1939 Earl Carroll Theater.

New York's Times Square set the neon standard in the 1930s. At night it was alive with the movement of headlights and taillights, and the radiating light from stores and cafes. The neon gave animation to the words and images of advertising: Capitol records, Mr. Peanut, A&P Coffees, Miss Youth Form ("aristocrat of slips"), Warner Brothers Strand. The abstract frames of the theater marquees glowed in Moderne or floral neon.

Times Square neon was a radical urban retrofit. It used neon like pen and ink, emphasizing thin, two-dimensional lines. Urban Times Square was, in effect, a brick and stone canyon that glowed with reflected and radiant light. Shards of light, color, and slogans splashed incongruously over the elegant stone and brick facades of Classicist buildings. Signs were scaled to be seen from across the street, and animation was timed to be visible to a pedestrian.

Twenty-five years later Fremont Street would take the neon city even further, turning the signs into the architecture itself. But in the 1930s Fremont Street was, like other Main Streets, still a distant provincial cousin of Times Square. Only at the end of the decade did the wattage pick up. The Hotel Apache began with a single horizontal sign extending from the third floor. The Frontier Club, Boulder Club, Las Vegas Club, and Sal Sagev Hotel all had large vertical signs with modified zigzag modern crests reaching no more than ten feet above the roofline. Each spelled out the club's name. The vaguely streamlined sign

♥

LAS VEGAS CLUB, c. 1934.
LAS VEGAS WAS STILL UN-SELF-CONSCIOUS.

for the late 1930s Frontier Club between First and Second was the most elaborate stylistically. The two tiers of lettering and the letters of the club were separated by horizontal lines. The Boulder Club began with a sign barely ten feet tall, later replaced with another standing a good story above the roofline. The Northern Club first used a single vertical vane, or pylon, sign, but later added a marquee angled out to be visible from car and sidewalk. Trimmed in neon, it featured a good poker hand and a sunburst. El Portal Theater and the Hotel Apache had signs on metal frameworks floating against the sky.

Only the number of signs, and the fact that they advertised roulette and keno, distinguished Fremont Street's neon from the signs in urban entertainment districts elsewhere. There was little unique about the neon city at this point. Though the city had boosters, a wide disinterest in redefining Las Vegas as a tourist mecca is confirmed in the 1940 *WPA Guide to Nevada, The Silver State*: "No cheap and easily parodied slogans have been adopted to publicize the city, no attempt has been made to introduce pseudo-romantic architectural themes, or to give artificial glamour and gai-

♣

BOULDER CLUB, C. 1940.
THE TYPICAL FREMONT STREET SAWDUST JOINT OF THIS PERIOD WAS A HIGH-CEILINGED STOREFRONT CRAMMED WITH GAMING TABLES AND A BAR. A BINGO LOUNGE STOOD AT THE REAR. NEON WAS USED FOR INDOOR LIGHTING.

ety. Las Vegas is itself—natural and therefore very appealing to people with a very wide variety of interests."

As Las Vegas became more savvy about the potential of a tourist economy, it began to exploit its western heritage more consciously. One variation on the motel was the dude ranch, a three-dimensional version of the Hollywood cowboy movie. Many divorce seekers met their six-week residency requirement by living at these ranches. Several working ranches near Las Vegas were converted for recreational use, where city folk could rest, relax, and enjoy a comfortable median between rough ranch life and city comforts. The Mormon fort abandoned in 1858 became Las Vegas Ranch in 1905, with tent cabins, a dance hall, and a pool created by damming a creek; the site is now at the corner of Las Vegas Boulevard North and Washington Avenue. The Kyle Ranch north of Las Vegas likewise converted to the dude ranch business in the 1920s, becoming the Boulderado. Other dude ranches were the Twin Lakes (now the Nevada State Museum and Historical Society) and the Bar W. Cowboy movie star Hoot Gibson opened the D-4-C in 1946 on Spring Mountain Road west of the Los Angeles Highway.

♠ ♦ ♣ ♥

THE COMPLETION OF the great dam in 1936 put the Las Vegas economy into a slump as construction workers went elsewhere for jobs. But as 1940 approached, the first phase of the building of Las Vegas drew to a close with an unexpected influx of out-of-towners. The cushy days for Los Angeles gamblers ended when reform candidate Fletcher Bowron won the mayor's race in late 1938 in the midst of a municipal scandal and began cleaning house. A number of gamblers did not wait to be swept out of town. One of them, Guy McAfee, a major gambling operator and also, not coincidentally, a police captain and commander of the vice squad, bought the Pair-O-Dice Club in 1939. It was one of the few casinos (the 1943 Players Club was another) already located on the Los Angeles Highway next to a few billboards and gas stations. McAfee would later rename this road the Strip in fond memory of the Sunset Strip. He "envisioned a gambling palace to replace the cheap old-fash-

CHAMBER OF COMMERCE BROCHURE, 1939. WESTERN WONDERS, MARRIAGE, AND DIVORCE WERE ALL EQUAL WITH GAMBLING AS LAS VEGAS ATTRACTIONS IN THE 1930s.

ioned flea pits with one pair of dice and a greasy deck of cards," wrote Las Vegas lawyer Paul Ralli in 1953. Renaming it the 91 Club, McAfee and his associates applied their operational expertise and merchandising skill in running this and other profitable, popular gambling establishments aimed at the Southern California market. He remained a respected public fixture for years.

Close on McAfee's heels came the more insidious influence of organized crime. Benjamin "Bugsy" Siegel saw the profit in taking over the Las Vegas race wires that reported race track results from around the country. Representing the Capone syndicate's Trans-America Wire Service, he muscled out the Continental Press Service and gained part ownership of several Fremont Street clubs including the Pioneer Club.

As 1940 approached, Uncle Sam once again stepped in as Las Vegas' fairy godfather. Fearing an attack on Atlantic Coast industrial centers and the threat of the Japanese Empire to the Pacific Coast, President Franklin D. Roosevelt's administration began to parcel out air bases and critical war industries among the more easily defended western states. Las Vegas got the Basic Magnesium, Inc., plant near Henderson and an air training station to the north. Both brought workers and soldiers whose paychecks took up the slack left when Boulder Dam workers departed. Las Vegas found itself with the two new industries—recreation and defense—which would shape western cities throughout the rest of the century. Fremont Street boomed.

*Ours was the first and will doubtless be the last party
of whites to visit this profitless locale.*

LIEUTENANT JOSEPH CHRISTMAS IVES, COLORADO RIVER EXPEDITION, 1857

2

The Early West in Modern Splendor: 1941—1945

MYTH ENSHRINES BENJAMIN Siegel as the Pierre L'Enfant of Las Vegas. Siegel's Flamingo Hotel, says the myth, established the pattern of landmark luxury resorts strung along a highway just as L'Enfant laid out the grand monuments of Washington, D.C., along its radial boulevards.

But if anyone can be given credit for starting the still-unnamed Las Vegas Strip on its way, it is Thomas Hull, Los Angeles hotel magnate. In 1941, five years before Siegel's Flamingo opened, Hull and his architect, Wayne McAllister, opened El Rancho Vegas, the first lavish motor hotel on Route 91, known as the Los Angeles Highway when it passed the city limits. Before El Rancho, the highway was dotted with a handful of scattered casinos, billboards, and gas stations, and included a radio station. The hotel established a pattern of roadside landmarks, vistas, and signs that broke with the tradition of downtown Las Vegas hotels and realized a vision that would mold the city's current form.

City planning was the last thing on Tom Hull's mind, of course. What he liked about the Los Angeles Highway was that it wasn't downtown. On the strip he could buy plenty of inexpensive land to spread out his new hotel. He also would have plenty of space for parking the cars that pulled into the hotel from the highway after the seven-hour drive from Los Angeles. Because his site sat just beyond city limits, he would be free of city taxes. Similar reasoning had convinced businesses to locate on commercial strips elsewhere in the country. Although El Rancho was not unusual compared with other motels and resorts in the West, it introduced two major elements to the development of the Las

Vegas style: the motel form and an architectural theme.

Thomas E. Hull was the managing director of Los Angeles' Hollywood-Roosevelt, Hollywood Plaza, and Mayfair hotels, Fresno's Hotel Californian, and Sacramento's Hotel Senator in the late 1930s. He also operated two El Rancho motels, El Rancho Fresno and El Rancho Sacramento. Both provided a template for the newest motel in Nevada; though more informal than Hull's in-town hotels, they had amenities including restaurants and entertainment.

For El Rancho Vegas, Hull selected Los Angeles architect Wayne McAllister, who had designed the other El Ranchos. Although a facile and imaginative designer working in both modern and historical styles, McAllister was never listed among the well-known Los Angeles architects of his day. He was a commercial architect with no formal training. Yet his Spanish-style buildings were rich and varied, comparable to the work of the elite Los Angeles historicist architects Gordon Kaufmann, Roland Coate, and Wallace Neff. McAllister's experience with casinos from the design of the successful 1931 Spanish-style Agua Caliente racetrack and hotel in Tijuana also recommended him to Hull. McAllister was also well known among Los Angeles restaura-

♠

FREMONT STREET FROM UNION PACIFIC STATION, c. 1942.

THE FIRST GLIMPSE OF LAS VEGAS FOR VISITORS ARRIVING BY TRAIN WAS FREMONT STREET. WRITER J. B. JACKSON CALLED SUCH URBAN AVENUES OF NEON AND AMUSEMENTS THE "STRANGER'S PATH." THE TURF CLUB REPLACED THE NORTHERN CLUB IN 1940.

PIONEER
CLUB
BAR
LAS VEGA
HOTEL
CLUB
HOTEL
Las Vegas
BAR
BAR
TURF Club
COCKTAIL BAR

◆

LEFT: **EL RANCHO VEGAS, c. 1941, WAYNE McALLISTER.** THE CASUAL RAMBLE OF EL RANCHO'S BUILDINGS CLEARLY REVEAL ITS MOTOR COURT ANCESTRY. THE FIRST HOTEL ON THE LOS ANGELES HIGHWAY (LATER KNOWN AS THE STRIP) WAS A LUSH OASIS SET IN THE ROADSIDE DESERT. FROM A DISTANCE, THE LOW-SLUNG BUILDINGS WERE INVISIBLE EXCEPT FOR THE TRADEMARK WINDMILL AND THE GAS STATION.

RIGHT: **BUNGALOWS, EL RANCHO VEGAS, c. 1941, WAYNE McALLISTER.** THOUGH THE MAIN BUILDING WAS RANCH-HOUSE RUSTIC, EL RANCHO'S ORIGINAL MOTEL BUNGALOWS SHARED THE THICK ADOBE-STYLE WALLS AND ARCHES OF SPANISH COLONIAL STYLE.

teurs for downtown's Mike Lyman's restaurant, the Renaissance Revival Biltmore Bowl, and Wilshire Boulevard's Zebra Room.

McAllister's modern work in Los Angeles is even more impressive, considering the standards set by architects R. M. Schindler and Richard Neutra. McAllister designed several polished streamlined drive-in restaurants for the Simon's and Herbert's chains, which were, functionally and theoretically, superb modern architecture. They attracted the critical eye of hungry drivers and the eminent historian Henry-Russell Hitchcock alike. In 1940, when El Rancho was being designed, Hitchcock wrote that McAllister's Van De Kamp's in Glendale represented "a very model of what exposition or resort architecture ought to be, light, gay, open, well executed and designed to be as effective by night as by day." Reflecting a common condescension toward commercial architects, Hitchcock unfortunately attributed this imaginative piece of architecture to only an "anonymous" architect. But his words were prophetic of the car-oriented architecture that

was to evolve from McAllister's designs of the 1930s.

Hull and McAllister first proposed a hotel for Las Vegas in 1938. The 160-acre site was two miles east of the center of town, off the Strip near the current Burnham Avenue and East Sahara Avenue. Clearly conceived in size and style as a successor to McAllister's rambling Spanish-style Agua Caliente, it would have been built on the edge of a plateau facing the desert scenery. A pyramid-topped tower marked the arches of the entry porch. As a self-contained destination resort, it made no inflection to the car or highway. Eighty rooms angled out in a V on the south side; an irregular collection of tiled-roof wings on the north side contained restaurant, lounge, and casino/lobby. Intended to attract a clientele as well-heeled as Agua Caliente's, the resort was aimed at "such wealthy centers as Oklahoma City, Dallas and Houston" as well as Los Angeles, stated the prospectus. Because of the fine weather, it continued, "many wealthy easterners who heretofore have patronized Florida may be expected to take advantage of the many attractions which this resort will offer. The combination of a fine hotel with a magnificent gambling casino creates an exceptional opportunity for profits."

Even with half the projected $500,000 budget coming from a federal Redevelopment Finance Corporation loan, Hull and McAllister couldn't get financing. Locals thought the resort too lavish; Los Angeles casino kingpin Nola Hahn and other experienced gamblers doubted that legal gambling could be profitable. Since constructing a full-fledged resort was too expensive, Hull decided to build a scaled-down version modeled on his El Rancho motels, financed by Texas connections and supported politically by local businessmen, headed by car dealer James

Cashman. It would be placed, like most motels, on the highway. Las Vegans were shocked at the move away from downtown. Breaking the tradition of downtown hotels and borrowing from the relaxed atmosphere and easy car accessibility of the roadside motel, El Rancho was a vision that was to change Las Vegas.

When El Rancho Vegas opened April 3, 1941, the Los Angeles Highway outside city limits was borderland, neither city nor country, marked by San Francisco Street (later Sahara Avenue). Los Angeles was three hundred miles to the west, and the desert in between was broken by only a few small towns offering a chance to stop for gas and a Coke. Las Vegas–bound travelers grew accustomed to the distant silhouettes of brown and red mountains mostly untouched by vegetation until billboards and a few small casinos along the two-lane highway heralded the approaching city.

For travelers driving north toward town, the first glimpse of El Rancho was of the gas station, included to encourage people to stop. Beyond that was the hotel's simple sign, lifted on stone pillars. A white wooden fence ran alongside the highway; the pool was visible behind a wooden trellis, palms, and shrubs. The distinctive landmark was a tall neon-trimmed windmill tower with "El Rancho Vegas" painted and outlined in orange neon on all sides. The main buildings were set back on the property.

El Rancho was lavish by Las Vegas standards. The Hotel Apache on Fremont Street was considered fancy, but it was still a standard downtown hotel. The dude ranches were western in style, but quaint rusticity was part of their charm. El Rancho's spaciousness, the outdoor pool and sunning areas, the privacy of the bungalows, and the green lawns amid the desert constituted luxurious rusticity.

Compared with Hull and McAllister's first hotel proposal, the completed El Rancho was low and rambling with varied rooflines, arbors, and trellises spread over seven acres. Stone chimneys highlighted board and batten siding. The ranch style echoed the other El Ranchos. It was "a sprawling group of haciendalike cottages built around a central cafe, night club and casino. Instead of hiding its glittering swimming pool in some patio, they stuck it in their show window, smack on Route 91," reported the *Saturday Evening Post.*

The lobby, casino, and showroom in the main building, with interiors also by McAllister, were in the wood ranch style; the room wings were stucco Spanish bungalow style. Stylistically the complex was not unusual. Rural simplicity was a favored conceit in Hollywood. Hotels, even gas stations, used the same motifs. Los Angeles' Farmer's Market, built in 1934, had used the ranch/farm style, including a windmill. In the same era, architect Cliff May's first ranch houses also used overtly rustic elements like rambling, shingled rooflines and board and batten walls like those at El Rancho.

♣

LEFT: **CHUCK WAGON, EL RANCHO VEGAS, C. 1941, WAYNE McALLISTER.** STAINLESS STEEL AND NEON WERE MIXED WITH WOOD PANELING AND ROMANTIC WESTERN MURALS IN EL RANCHO'S OLD WEST–STYLE BUFFET.

RIGHT: **CASINO, EL RANCHO VEGAS, C. 1941, WAYNE McALLISTER.** SPINDLE LEGS ON THE CRAPS TABLES AND HEAVY WOOD TRUSSES ORNAMENTED WITH NATIVE AMERICAN DESIGN MOTIFS BROUGHT THE SPLENDOR OF THE OLD WEST TO GAMBLING. IT WAS THE FIRST THEMED HOTEL IN LAS VEGAS.

♥

Inside, El Rancho reflected the rustic motifs of ranch houses and bunkhouses. The casino, restaurant/showroom, and shops had log beam trusses, wood paneling, fringed leather drapes, and western paintings. Yoke chandeliers hung from the plank ceiling. Outside, El Rancho had green lawns, wood fences, a sundeck, stables, and private bungalows. "The Rancho somehow has managed to make the riveter, the carpenter and the truck driver at home in overalls in the same rooms with men and women in smart sports clothes, with an eloping Lana Turner posing for news photographers. . . . No resort is likely to succeed in Vegas that doesn't accomplish this democracy," reported the *Saturday Evening Post*.

None of El Rancho's signage was large. As the only hotel on the highway, it did not have to be. Two signs stood at roadside. One, at the corner of the property, spelled out "El Rancho" in channel letters sitting atop a low log. The other was a square board of painted metal, also outlined in neon, and stood in front of the pool announcing "Fine Foods, Casino." The windmill stood above the main entry on the side of the building. All were outlined in neon. They lacked the flamboyance that came to be associated with Las Vegas, but they had started something.

El Rancho opened with fifty rooms and Hull soon added sixty more. In 1942 Hull sold part of his interest due to management problems. Under a succession of owners, including future Desert Inn owner Wilbur Clark, and finally under Beldon Katleman in 1947, El Rancho became a major resort. Although it was not astonishing compared with resorts in Palm Springs, Santa Barbara, or Phoenix, Las Vegans were amazed that something so lavish and far from downtown could succeed.

By 1941 Las Vegas had at least twenty-six motor courts of its own, mostly along the stretch of Route 91 within city limits known as Fifth Street. With names like the Chief Court, Autel, and Gateway Auto Court, they were typical of the motels to be found on the roads into many other towns.

El Rancho set the pattern of the large highway resort hotel. With its opening, the builders of Las Vegas varied the motel archetype a bit: the sign was expanded, the lobby was enlarged to include a casino, and the room wings were surrounded by recreational facilities and lush planting. A bigger budget, a slightly different program, but a motel nonetheless.

When another out-of-towner, Texas theater chain owner R. E. Griffith, decided to duplicate El Rancho's success, the mold was cast. Also a large motel, also on the strip, Griffith's Last Frontier was even more richly themed in the casual western mode.

Griffith and his son-in-law, architect William J. Moore, had stopped at the new El Rancho on a business trip in 1941, decided it was a great idea, and thought they could do even better. Buying property a mile south of El Rancho, on the site occupied by the 91 Club, they built the Las Vegas Strip's second hotel resort, opening in 1942. Moore, a 1936 graduate in architecture from Oklahoma A. & M., had designed theaters in Oklahoma and Texas.

For the Last Frontier, Moore designed a sprawling rancho on 5 acres, though the property included 175 acres. The rural-style shake eaves over the entry were lined with neon lettering bracketed by western scenes painted on sheet metal. The contrast between rustic wood shingles and sleek neon visually telegraphed the slogan of the Last Frontier, "The Early West in Modern Splendor," matched by the appearance of Sophie Tucker in sequined chaps. It was a convincing image of a western civilization blessed with the conveniences of modern times but not cursed by modern imagery. It clearly followed in the tra-

♠

The Last Frontier's lobby, emphasizing natural materials, had a hexagonal stone chimney rising two stories through rough-hewn beams. Chandeliers made of wagon wheels hung overhead. Moore borrowed liberally from the forms of meeting houses, saloons, hunting lodges, ranches, and even bunkhouses and barns. The unpainted wood, the use of hand-crafted artifacts as ornament, and the ruggedly self-conscious simplicity also tied the style to the Arts and Crafts bungalows that flourished at the turn of the century, when Navajo rugs adorned many a Pasadena bungalow's parlor. A trophy room, the Horn Room, featured animal heads. The Ramona Room, the dining room/showroom, held six hundred seats. Cow horns were fixed on all bedsteads. Completing the theme, stagecoaches picked up guests at the airport, pack trips could be arranged, and a stable stood out back. In spirit if not size, the Last Frontier rivaled the great rustic park resorts of the West: the 1904 Old Faithful Inn by Robert Reamer in Yellowstone, the 1926 Ahwanee by Gilbert Stanley Underwood in Yosemite, the 1934 Bright Angel Lodge by Mary Colter at Grand Canyon.

The main thematic element, conceived by Moore and added in 1947, was Last Frontier Village. Using the collection of Nevada antique collector Robert Caudill, called Doby Doc, Moore re-created a small western village, with entire buildings taken from older towns,

dition of the Harvey Houses of forty years before.

Where El Rancho rambled like a motor court, the Last Frontier was a single sprawling building with 107 rooms. Several distinct but connected segments gave the facade the appearance of a main street from an Old West town. The lobby portion was the tallest, with a broad shingled roof and a porch stretching across its front. South of that was the Ramona Room, faced in stone, with French doors that let out onto a patio ringed in wagon wheels. The Carrillo Room, named for actor Leo Carrillo, the Cisco Kid's sidekick, was an octagonal tower that had been part of the Club 91 that originally occupied the site. The Gay Nineties Bar next to that had a porch held up with natural logs. The two-story room wings containing the 107 rooms had double-loaded corridors and covered garages for cars.

Yet the Last Frontier was still a motel at heart. Front and center, right on the highway, was the pool, a splashing oasis that was the hotel's best advertisement to road-weary drivers. Surrounded by a split rail fence, the pool was contained in a corral that linked it to the hotel's theme. Parking for four hundred cars was provided.

Like El Rancho, the Last Frontier had modest roadside signs. Low signs styled in a rustic board typeface stood waist-high on logs at the edge of the property where travelers could see the sign as they approached. The two resorts did not engage in a sign competition; even at two stories, the buildings stood out in the desert landscape.

♣

LOBBY, LAST FRONTIER, 1942, WILLIAM MOORE. A LUXURIOUS RUSTICITY THAT ECHOED HUNTING LODGES, NATIONAL PARK HOTELS, AND RANCH HOUSES BROUGHT AN IMAGE OF SPLENDOR TO THE WILDERNESS.

BELOW (LEFT): **CASINO, LAST FRONTIER, 1942, WILLIAM MOORE.** AMERICANIZING MONTE CARLO, LAS VEGAS REPLACED FORMAL WEAR AND ARISTOCRATIC MANNERS WITH BOLO TIES AND WESTERN STITCHERY.

including a jail, a Joss house for the Chinese who worked on the railroad, and a mining train. Ten years before Disneyland's Frontierland or Knott's Berry Farm's ghost town, Las Vegas offered an experience of the Old West for tourists in search of the real thing. With scrub brush lapping at the rear door and the distant mountains as backdrop, the Last Frontier packaged the Old West in scenographic terms.

This was theme architecture: the thorough depiction of a particular historical era or geographical area in the architecture, ornament, costumes, and service of the hotel. The re-creation does not have to be accurate; it usually tells us more about the era that produced it than the era that it is purported to depict. Often nostalgic, it is a way for the fast-moving present to achieve a level of comfort by surrounding itself with a known past. As Las Vegas grew, it was to become an entire city of themes.

The motel archetype, organized along the linear highway and given meaning by themes: this was the seed planted by El Rancho Vegas. In the next decades it would grow into a new type of city. Though not unique to Las Vegas, there it would take on exaggerated and vivid form. Only in the western desert could such development enjoy the freedom from cultural precedent and physical infrastructure that would allow it to blossom. Strip hotels were free to respond to commercial requirements. In Las Vegas and in other cities, the center of urban gravity would shift from the established downtowns to these new suburbs.

Such was the modest but upscale birth of the Strip. With the approach of war, its evolution would be arrested; no more resorts would be built outside of town until 1946. In the early 1940s, the pendulum swung back to Fremont Street, the old downtown. It was ready to boom.

Downtown Las Vegas circa 1941 was a combination of railroad town and old frontier town. Its western quality was understated. The florid interpretations of western tourism seen in El Rancho Vegas had

not yet hit town. The war boom pumped money into the downtown casinos, which allowed them to grow by absorbing neighboring bakeries, Western Union offices, and other casinos; except for the casinos, the commercial mix had been similar to any town of its size in the 1930s. Fifty years later this consolidation would result in single casinos stretching across entire blocks and encroaching on blocks on either side of Fremont Street. Ill-prepared to cope with the car, downtown faced a major parking problem during the wartime boom. Parallel parking was replaced with diagonal parking until parking was banned entirely from the casino district, and Fremont Street through the casino district became one-way.

"Las Vegas keeps to the traditions of western towns by having one main street that shoots the works," wrote Erle Stanley Gardner in 1941. "A few cash-and-carry grocers and businesses . . . hang on to the side streets. Two main districts branch out at each end of this main street; one of them a two-mile long collection of tourist camps containing some of the best air-conditioned auto cabins in the country. At the other end, like the arm of a big Z, is the stretch of houses where women sit around—waiting. The length of the main street is sprinkled with gambling casinos, eating places, hotels, drugstores, and saloons. Virtually every form of gambling runs wide-open."

The downtown casinos were sawdust joints. Photographs from the 1930s show serious gamblers, mostly men, around the poker and craps tables, but bejeweled women were commonly reported in Fremont Street casinos sitting next to workers from Hoover Dam. Without the pools and floor shows of the Strip's classier carpet joints, Fremont was a more concentrated gambling experience.

In the 1930s "bettors risked only small sums, and observers mostly agreed that the businesses were small, even harmless. . . . Local residents prided themselves not on the economic success of gaming but rather on its upright character," writes historian John Findlay in *People of Chance*. It took outsiders to show Las Vegas a more cutthroat and profitable means of operation. After a decade of hesitant promotion as "a minor league Reno," in the words of the *Saturday Evening Post*, the city finally became a major resort when World War II brought in large numbers of customers. "There are bigger war booms than Vegas', but not relatively, nor any other so gaudy," believed the *Post*.

One sign of Fremont Street's approaching prosperity came with the construction of the Spanish-style, fifty-nine-room El Cortez hotel and casino in 1941, built by Los Angeles contractor Marion Hicks with John Grayson for $250,000. Located several blocks east of the old center, the all-new building was bigger than most Fremont Street clubs, which were remodeled storefronts on fifty-foot lots. The hotel's massing was asymmetrical; an arcade of Moorish arches ran along one side. Bricks with weeping mortar faced the building. A large sign was lifted on a steel frame over the red tile roof.

The gamblers squeezed out of Los Angeles after 1938 by the reform mayor (and, to an extent, by Ben Siegel) brought with them experience in running profitable gaming clubs. Several of them, including 91 Club owner Guy McAfee, opened the Pioneer Club at the corner of Fremont and First streets in 1942. Thirteen gambling houses were added to Las Vegas proper, and the same number opened in the county during the war, reported the *Saturday Evening Post*.

Unlike the old Northern Club or the modernistic Boulder Club, the Pioneer was consciously western in style, showing the influence of El Rancho and the Last Frontier; the suburban strip was already influencing the old central city. The Pioneer Club began in the existing three-story Beckley Building on the standard fifty-foot lot. An undistinguished version of the Mission Revival, the structure had a tile roofline and arches painted like eyebrows above the third floor. A geometric frieze was painted under the eaves for decoration. The Pioneer's vertical sign in Old West typeface was mounted well above the roofline; a side-

walk canopy held large lettering and pictures of a miner, a mule, and a Conestoga wagon.

The Pioneer started a sign trend and then had to run to keep up with it. When the Pioneer Club introduced cactus and covered wagons to its signage after 1942, western motifs were among a variety of images that appeared on signage. In quick succession, neon cacti were mounted to the corner of the Pioneer building, the mule and miner disappeared, and neon was added to the eyebrows on the facade. The corner sign sitting on top of the new sidewalk canopy was enlarged and repeated "Pioneer Club" for good measure. Sheet metal mountains were added to the canopy.

Over the decade postcards reveal a growing incrustation of neon tube lighting; neon seemed to be driving the architectural development of Fremont at this point. Casino owners and sign companies

VIVA LAS VEGAS

EL CORTEZ HOTEL, FREMONT AND SIXTH STREETS, 1941. LIKE TRAIN STATIONS AND RESORT HOTELS THROUGHOUT THE WEST, EL CORTEZ TOOK THE RAMBLING SPANISH STYLE INDIGENOUS TO THE REGION. IN 1951, THE GROUND FLOOR WAS "MODERNIZED," ADDING A NEON CANOPY BY YESCO AND BEZEL-FRAMED DISPLAY WINDOWS. THE EXTERIOR HAS REMAINED VIRTUALLY UNCHANGED SINCE THEN.

slowly escalated and accelerated the competition. Permanent sidewalk canopies, known in Las Vegas since 1905, became wider and served as frames for neon under, over, and along the marquees. Signs were scaled to compete with neighboring buildings and to draw in passersby on the sidewalk.

Although neon was common throughout the country in the 1940s, Las Vegas' concentration of entertainment business within a few blocks put an emphasis on brightness, eye-grabbing images, and visual density. The Pioneer's large sign prompted the Boulder Club to update its sign with a larger one. So did the Las Vegas Club. Fremont Street is where neon ignited in Las Vegas. In comparison, the modest neon windmill on El Rancho and the neon lettering on the Last Frontier seemed lost in the vast space along the highway.

Other new casinos opened in 1942. Tony Cornero closed down his gambling boat off Santa Monica, California, the SS *Rex*, under pressure from California attorney general Earl Warren in August 1939, but then attempted to relaunch it on the inland sea as a club, the

SS *Rex*, in the Hotel Apache in 1944. Because of questions about its backers, however, it failed to receive a gambling license. The Monte Carlo replaced the Turf Club in 1945, adding a Moderne sign in rounded letters set on a box grid, and an ornate marquee with "Monte Carlo" in script.

Cornero wasn't the only underworld figure to appear in Las Vegas. Benjamin Siegel, known to press and peers as Bugsy, had been sent by the Capone-Luciano syndicate to oversee Los Angeles operations in 1937. Siegel had quickly made friends in the film community. Though hot tempered, he possessed a charm, and frequently an owner's percentage, which made him welcome in Los Angeles' fanciest nightclubs. He was attracted to Las Vegas in the summer of 1941 to establish his syndicate's Trans-America Wire Service over the existing Continental Press Service. Race wires reported to bookies the results of horse races across the nation. With associate Moe Sedway, Siegel would often demand a percentage of the casino. Reportedly he became part owner of the Frontier Club and other Fremont Street establishments before buying El Cortez in early 1946.

Though many smaller clubs moved in and out on a regular

UNION PACIFIC STATION, 1940. THE TRAIN STATION WAS THE BEST EXAMPLE OF THE STREAMLINE MODERNE IN LAS VEGAS. IT REPLACED THE THIRTY-YEAR-OLD SPANISH-STYLE STATION.

basis, the major clubs grew. Even before Pearl Harbor, the Apache, Northern, Boulder, and Las Vegas clubs expanded into neighboring storefronts and bars to make bigger and more spacious casinos. Wayne McAllister remodeled and opened up the interior of El Cortez in 1946 for Siegel's syndicate. Pushing through exterior walls but restricted by the low ceiling heights of the old structures, casino interiors became distinctively large and low rooms. With the clusters of gaming tables and the people huddled over them, and the chrome glint of rows upon rows of slot machines, the casinos began to create a visual texture of great complexity but overall uniformity. The *kerchunk* of slot machines added an aural texture. Fremont casinos, unlike those on the Strip at this time, stood right on the sidewalk, and the doors—often glass, as in the modernized Las Vegas Club—could be pulled back to allow the casino space to flow outside under the neon marquees, across the street, and into another casino—an unbroken public room combining inside and outside.

In the view of many boosters, their town was still a product in need of packaging, Las Vegas' version of urban planning. "Still a Frontier Town," boasted the Chamber of Commerce. This town born in the twentieth century sought to reach back to a perceived past of western hospitality and personal freedom to which it felt heir. One local paper tempted visitors "to throw off the shackles which chain him in practically every other community in America. Here freedom is a living, breathing thing." The western theme of El Rancho and Last Frontier was impressive enough to rally boosters' efforts. By 1944 they were considering making the western style mandatory throughout Fremont Street. Though the idea was never formally adopted, many casinos voluntarily got on the bandwagon. A prospector was paid to stand with his donkey in front of one downtown hotel to regale tourists.

Several popular architectural elements of the western town were key: false fronts, covered sidewalks, names referring to people (Fremont, Pioneer) or places (Boulder) associated in the popular imagination with the West. Saloons and gambling halls were an important part of the mythic West; Las Vegas could offer tourists something very much like the real thing. Even draped in neon, this vernacular design language was respected. Not coincidentally these changes arrived with the growing influence of Los Angeles, with which Las Vegas has had a

symbiotic relationship. Local defense workers were augmented by tourists arriving from Los Angeles to gamble and play during the war years. Movies had made Angelenos conscious of imagery and packaging; now they could expand it into a pragmatic approach to urban design using theme architecture and neon signs. An ad hoc vernacular evolved, driven by pragmatic commercial demands to promote the casinos.

Fremont Street became a greenhouse for neon signs. Intramural sign competition would lead to excesses and innovations that would make Las Vegas a city of signs and light. Though the boom of the early 1940s spurred Fremont Street more than it did the new highway hotels, the crowding and parking problems downtown underscored the advantages of the roadside site. There, through the commercial vernacular processs, the resort casinos had begun to adapt the forms of the strip and the motel. El Rancho and the Last Frontier were more than motels; they were themed places that borrowed regional history as a way to focus a vacationer's experience. It was a modest start, but the first of many steps that would result in today's Strip City.

♥

PIONEER CLUB, 1942. LIKE MOST FREMONT STREET CLUBS, THE PIONEER REMODELED AN EXISTING COMMERCIAL BUILDING (THE BECKLEY) INTO A CASINO, ADDING A SIDEWALK CANOPY AND GLASS DOORS THAT FACILITATED ENTRY.

Show me the ultimate reason for these matters; show me the sublime presence of the highest spiritual cause lurking, as always it does lurk, in the suburbs and extremities of nature.

RALPH WALDO EMERSON, THE AMERICAN SCHOLAR, 1837

3

A Place in the Sun: 1946—1957

AN INVISIBLE LINE cuts through the barren strata and empty basins of the Mojave Desert fifty miles east of Baker, California. It has nothing to do with physical geography. It is a figment of the bureaucratic imagination, fixed in Washington, D.C., during the Civil War. This arbitrary line gave the state legislature of Nevada the right to make laws to the east of the line. The legislature of Nevada used that right to legalize gambling in 1931. That, in turn, made possible the phantasms of Las Vegas architecture.

One of those startling visions rose into the view of travelers just before they arrived at the Las Vegas city limits in late 1946. After miles of trackless desert, they saw a thin metal slab with "Hotel Flamingo" written vertically, accompanied by a flamingo sketched in neon. The building below it was long and low, the landscaping like an oasis. Overall, the appearance was of an unusually lavish roadside motel. Greeting travelers on the southeast corner was a sign with script letters hugging the ground. Another sign with an attraction board featuring the name of the week's starring personality stood on two legs marking the driveway. On top of the sign was a Gruen clock, making an odd roadside version of the clocktower of courthouse squares. It was designed by Hermon Boernge of the Young Electric Sign Company. A long unbroken ashlar stone wall stood to the right.

If you thought you had left the sophistication of Beverly Hills behind, you suddenly rediscovered it here in the desert. The lines of the Flamingo Hotel were horizontal, sharp, and modern like the newest drive-in restaurants; lining the roof and silhouetted against the sky were the steel channels of neon lettering. The sign here said "Casino Lounge Restaurant," whereas a drive-in would have read "Hamburgers Shakes Ham 'n' Eggs." But the jutting wood fascia, sharp as a knife, sheltering a wide porch and a wall of plate glass, could have been an entry to Romanoff's or any restaurant on La Cienega's Restaurant Row in Los Angeles. The base of the sign pylon, to the left of the doors, echoed the fascia in a wood zigzag. A canvas awning led to a second entrance framed in the deep-set bezel frame typical of the latest angular Moderne.

Rome has a legend about Romulus and Remus. Las Vegas has a legend about the Flamingo. As with most legends, the truth is hidden beneath layers of colorful fiction. It was not, as is often believed, the first resort on the Strip; El Rancho Vegas had been built five years before. Benjamin "Bugsy" Siegel, the Flamingo's owner, did not invent Las Vegas single-handedly; he had not even started the Flamingo. Yet this original, simpler Flamingo came to be forgotten with the arrival of the big neon signs and fabulously tasteless hotels that characterized Las Vegas style in the 1950s and 1960s. Even Tom Wolfe, a discerning critic of popular culture, identified a later, flashier Flamingo with a tower covered in neon champagne

♣

FLAMINGO HOTEL, 1947, GEORGE VERNON RUSSELL. RUSSELL, BILLY WILKERSON, AND BENJAMIN SIEGEL TRANSPORTED A HOLLYWOOD NIGHTCLUB TO THE NEVADA DESERT. THE NEON FLAMINGO ON TOP OF THE PYLON WAS ADDED AFTER THE 1946 OPENING. THE MAIN ENTRY IS TO THE RIGHT.

♥

**FLAMINGO HOTEL,
1946, GEORGE VERNON
RUSSELL.**
WOOD, ASHLAR, AND EX-
OTIC PLANTING SET THE
SOPHISTICATED FLAMINGO
APART FROM THE RUSTIC EL
RANCHO AND LAST
FRONTIER. IT WAS HARDLY
THE GARISH NEON IMAGE
FOR WHICH LAS VEGAS
WAS TO BECOME FAMOUS.

as Bugsy's original, but when that sign was built in 1953, Siegel had been dead six years.

What the legend does not exaggerate is the Flamingo's importance. It created a significant new sophisticated market for Las Vegas; it opened the Strip to a wider range of images in the service of making appealing places; it broke Las Vegas out of the public relations mold of a western town of modern splendor and set it on its way to being a mirror of the spectrum of American popular culture.

Critics and observers from the East Coast had difficulty grasping this new phenomenon. Casting around for a source for Las Vegas' informality, popularity, and flamboyance, they compared it with Miami, another resort with a warm climate and exuberant architecture. Tom Wolfe and others labeled Las Vegas and the Flamingo in particular as "Miami Modern" or "Miami Baroque," and the label stuck. The hotel's name, seeming to refer to the flamingo flock at Florida's Hialeah racetrack, added to the confusion. This is a fundamental misperception of the roots of Las Vegas. It is a western phenomenon, tied to the car, the suburban strip, and a postindustrial society emerging after World War II. Los Angeles, providing many of Las Vegas' architects and most of its customers in this period, was its model.

In fact, Miami Modern did not exist in 1946 when the Flamingo was designed. Modern public buildings there were relatively

chaste; the small resort hotels of Miami Beach then were Streamline Moderne. Their unmistakable curving corners, zigzag pylons, and stylized tropical friezes reflected the styles of the 1930s. They fronted on the sidewalk.

Morris Lapidus, the architect most identified with the Florida style, received his first Miami commission, the Sans Souci, in 1948, followed by the 1954 Eden Roc, the 1954 Fontainebleau, and the 1955 Americana. While owing more to modern South American precedents, Lapidus' hotels did share with Las Vegas hotels a sense of public drama and a modern vocabulary of swoops, woggles, cheese holes, bright colors, and dramatic nighttime illumination. But like Miami's 1947 Delano Hotel and others, Lapidus' designs reflected a genealogy that was urban and highrise, not roadside and motel. Neither did the Flamingo echo the International-Style-on-vacation designs of Caribbean resorts such as Edward Durrell Stone's 1946 El Panama Hotel in Panama, a Modernist rectangular block with a grilled facade and free-form walkway canopies.

The Flamingo combined two Western trends: the vernacular motel and the modern styles developing in Los Angeles. Like El Rancho and the Last Frontier, the Flamingo was a glorified motel, but it absorbed the modern styling and planning increasingly utilized by motels. "The popularity and financial success of the new motels has been so great, however, that. . . the motel has become a symbol of up-to-dateness, of informality and modern planning," reported Geoffrey Baker and Bruno Funaro, dean of the School of Architecture at Columbia University in 1955. Motels continued to be typified by long, low repetitive room units on a large piece of roadside property, but frequently grew to include two-story units. An outdoor corridor linked the rooms; this balcony overlooked either parking lot or pool. Railings and stairs offered decorative opportunities to convey the design's modernity. The pool (often with a slide to enlist children's votes in the family's motel selection process) became a roadside attraction. At a time when residential swimming pools were a symbol of wealth, anyone could enjoy the relaxation of a (mostly) private pool for the moderate cost of a night's lodging.

The simple, isolated motor courts of the 1930s were clearly evolving into something more sophisticated. They were also as familiar in America as the courthouse square or the skyscraper tower. Before

long they would be seen as the seeds of a new urban pattern recognized by one of the fathers of modern suburbia, mallmeister Victor Gruen, in *Architectural Record* in 1958: "These [motor] hotels will assume for suburban industrial, commercial and residential communities the same role first-class hotels play downtown."

The car shaped the Flamingo as it did any motel. Set back from the road, the casino was angled so that southbound traffic from downtown would have a full view of the main facade. A parking lot up front provided the frame for the low, rambling structure set in the middle of a large tract of land. The two-, three-, and four-story room wings formed a horseshoe protecting the pool in the middle. As at other motels, rooms also faced the parking lot for easy access. With 105 rooms, a health club, a gym, a steam room, tennis, handball, and squash courts, stables, trap shooting, and a nine-hole golf course, the Flamingo offered complete resort facilities. The grounds were lavishly planted with exotic species trucked in from Los Angeles nurseries to emphasize the oasis/mirage quality.

If the Flamingo's concept derived from the roadside vernacular, its style was from Los Angeles Modernism. There, in the late 1930s and early 1940s, architects had moved beyond the Streamline Moderne to incorporate the sculptural and spatial play of work by local avant-garde architects R. M. Schindler, Richard Neutra, and John Lautner.

The movie industry provided many of the willing and wealthy clients for this new style. The style could be seen in private homes and particularly in the public haunts of Hollywood's nightclubbing elite, at Romanoff's, Ciro's, Coffee Dan's, the Trocadero, the Mocambo. These designs often used dynamic geometric volumes—wedges, tilted planes—and natural materials—unpainted wood, brick, stone, glass, copper—which produced cleaner lines than the curvy Streamline Moderne. Ornament was either stylized Regency or the swoops and free forms of modern art. Compared with the static International Style popular in the East in the period, these designs were more dynamic. Los Angeles had evolved a casual and popular yet sophisticated modern architecture.

J. R. Davidson's Perino's restaurant appeared in Los Angeles in 1930; while related to the Streamline Moderne, it was clearly more controlled. R. M. Schindler designed the dynamic Sardi's on Hollywood Boulevard in 1932. Mainstream architect Gordon Kaufmann designed the Earl Carroll Theater, a 1938 landmark which clearly established distance from the Moderne in its preference for planar designs using exotic materials and imaginative neon. From society architect Douglas Honnold's office came the elegant Modernism of Romanoff's, and, from his chief designer, John Lautner, a series of early 1940s Coffee

Dan's restaurants that attracted the screen crowd.

Honnold's partner in the late 1930s was George Vernon Russell. He remodeled the Trocadero, originally an elegant farmhouse, for client Billy Wilkerson in 1936 into a sleek modernized version of the Hollywood Regency style. The 1940 Ciro's, also for Wilkerson, used a free-form canopy, screen grills, and square bezels in an early example of the late Moderne.

As owner of the *Hollywood Reporter*, Wilkerson could set fashions and then publicize them. His string of swank restaurants and nightclubs had all been successful, so during the early 1940s he decided to take the same Hollywood formula to Las Vegas. He was not the first; before the war, Los Angeles gambling czar Nola Hahn of the Clover Club had opened the Colony Club in Las Vegas off the Los Angeles Highway. "The Colony is as modernistic, as chi-chi, as sophisticated in decor as anything in New York," reported Wesley Stout in the *Saturday Evening Post*, but due partly to a poor location, it was short-lived.

In late 1945, Wilkerson purchased land on the west side of the Los Angeles Highway, about one mile south of the Last Frontier, reports historian Robert Lacey, biographer of Siegel's friend and associate Meyer Lansky. Wilkerson hired George Vernon Russell once again to design a casino and hotel that would translate the glamour of his Sunset Strip clubs to the desert. Construction began in Spring of 1946; but due to the high cost of materials immediately after the war, Wilkerson ran out of money.

To his rescue came a consortium of East Coast businessmen who could invest $1 million. They appeared legitimate, and agreed to

let Wilkerson retain one-third ownership and operational control. Only later did he learn that his new partners included Benjamin Siegel. Siegel, who moved comfortably in the fashionable Hollywood milieu, knew Wilkerson's plush Los Angeles clubs. After buying and selling El Cortez in 1946, he was looking for a new Las Vegas investment. Though their partnership began amicably, by December 1946 costs ballooned and Siegel began forcing Wilkerson out with threats. Wilkerson finally severed his connection in April 1947. Siegel took over the project, named the Flamingo Hotel, and it became his obsession as he convinced his suspicious underworld colleagues to bankroll the vision.

The truth of the Flamingo's birth stands in contrast to the legend, which places it in Siegel's rapturous desert revelation of an American Monte Carlo while his stupefied lieutenants stood by in the howling wasteland that was to become the Strip. But with El Rancho and the Last Frontier already in place, the idea of a hotel and casino on the Los Angeles Highway was not novel. For an energetic and stylish

◆

ABOVE: **FLAMINGO HOTEL, 1946, GEORGE VERNON RUSSELL.** THE BAR AND CASINO OF THE FLAMINGO HAD VIEWS TO THE POOL.

BELOW: **FLAMINGO HOTEL, GEORGE VERNON RUSSELL, 1952.** THE FLAMINGO PRESENTED A STARTLING VISION AMID THE DESERT WASHES. THE UNION PACIFIC TRACK CAN BE SEEN AT THE TOP OF THE IMAGE. A SMALL WEDDING CHAPEL STOOD TO THE RIGHT OF THE CASINO.

entrepreneur familiar with the L.A. gambling market, it would have been an easy step to see the possibilities of a market niche mixing gambling with glamour to appeal to the sizable L.A. population just three hundred miles down the highway.

To attract the upscale audience, the architecture was critical. El Rancho and the Last Frontier traded on Old West nostalgia. Russell gave Wilkerson and Siegel a building where Los Angeles high rollers would feel at home. He saw the desert not as a set for a western but as a blank slate on which anything could be written. It would be a major shift in the way the Las Vegas desert was perceived by tourists and the tourist industry. Though Siegel associates contacted Wayne McAllister (who politely declined due to concerns about overcoming material shortages), George Vernon Russell remained the Flamingo's architect.

Less than a year after V-J Day, building materials were still in short supply for civilian use; Siegel called on his connections to get the project built quickly. He also brought in Phoenix-based contractor Del Webb, whose association with Las Vegas continues to the present. Though Siegel drove his contractor at a breakneck speed, he demanded quality materials and quality construction for his landmark. Ed Reid and Ovid Demaris reported in *The Green Felt Jungle* that Siegel berated the architects and designers "at every turn, demanding things newer and rarer." Russell, however, remembered Siegel as a good client who was polite and always paid his bills, said Russell's son. "He was a remarkable character," reported Del Webb, "Tough, cold, and terrifying when he wanted to be—but at other times a very easy fellow to be around."

In design, the casino was casually asymmetrical, presenting two wings bridged by a long horizontal wedge of wood floating over a glass entry. A vertical sign pylon pinned down the wide, jutting canopy. Each layer of red cedar board was inset slightly from the one below to emphasize the horizontal line, a device used by Frank Lloyd Wright in the 1930s. The walls were reinforced concrete faced in green ashlar stone or stucco.

Inside the Flamingo was spacious and air-conditioned. A waterfall stood by the entry. The bar and casino formed a long room with windows angled to look out on the pool. Shocking pink leather-finish upholstery accented the soft greens of the wallpaper and carpet, "warm

tones that slug it out with the air conditioning," noted *The New Yorker's* A. J. Liebling in 1950. Walls of green stone from Utah and hanging V-shaped light troughs followed the oblique angles of the lobby. The banana-leaf wallpaper was complemented by ornamental branches and leaves surrounding the windows and a mirrored wall near the slot machines.

Beyond the cool panorama of the pool court, the room wing offered a backdrop, a three-story building of simple

♣

EL RANCHO VEGAS, WAYNE McALLISTER, 1952.
TO KEEP UP WITH THE RASH OF NEW RESORTS, EL RANCHO ENLARGED ITS SHOWROOM, RENAMING IT THE OPERA HOUSE, OPENED UP ITS ENTRY WITH MORE GLASS, AND ADDED—OF COURSE—MORE NEON.

♥

THUNDERBIRD HOTEL, 1948.

THE DESERT LITERALLY LAPPED AT THE BACK DOORS OF THE FIRST LAS VEGAS RESORTS. BROAD ROOFS HELPED MARK THE SITE IN THE ROADSIDE EXPANSE. IN THE DISTANCE CAN BE SEEN THE SHORT-LIVED RACETRACK ON THE SITE OF THE PRESENT LAS VEGAS HILTON. COMPARE THIS AERIAL VIEW WITH THE ONE IN CHAPTER FOUR.

THUNDERBIRD HOTEL, 1948.

NEON THUNDERBIRDS FLOCKED AROUND THE NEW HOTEL. THEIR NEON NATURALISM HELPED TO INTEGRATE SIGNAGE WITH ARCHITECTURE WHEN THE HOTEL'S OBSERVATION TOWER BECAME THEIR PERCH. THE THUNDERBIRD HAD THE FIRST PORTE COCHERE ON THE STRIP.

lines, stepping up to a fourth floor for Siegel's suite. Local architect Richard Stadelman designed this double-loaded room wing; he had also designed additions to El Rancho. The pool had scalloped sides and was surrounded by grass, palms, and lounge chairs, the motel-modern image of an oasis. A walkway with a roof cantilevered off the main building led to the pool.

The architecture had the elegant proportions of George Vernon Russell's work, balancing flat walls with detailed entries and windows accented by natural materials. It lacked the fineness of the best of Los Angeles Modern; it did not have the bold sculpturing of space, for example, of John Lautner's Coffee Dan's. But the Flamingo's casual openness, broad stretches of glass, and natural materials tied it to the style.

Some called the Flamingo a mobster vision of heaven, ignoring the involvement of true sophisticates like Wilkerson and Russell. But as Tom Wolfe pointed out in his 1964 *Esquire* article, "The important

thing about the building of Las Vegas is not that the builders were gangsters but that they were proles. . . . the first uneducated, prole-petty-burgher Americans to have enough money to build a monument to their style of life." Their taste reflected the sensibility of a newly prosperous class to which commercial architecture was appealing nationwide.

Siegel's $6 million vision outlived him. He was assassinated in June 1947, at age forty-two, after the Flamingo had been operating only a few months. The grand opening on December 26, 1946, featuring Jimmy Durante and Xavier Cugat (not Abbott and Costello, as the legend has it), was disastrous; the hotel rooms were unfinished and the Hollywood guests didn't arrive because of bad weather in Los Angeles. The Flamingo closed soon and a second opening was scheduled the next March when the ninety-three-room hotel was complete. It was better attended, and by May the Flamingo was turning a profit, though Siegel may have been skimming the profits for himself. With an eye to public relations, his murderers waited until he was well out of town, in Beverly Hills. Within a few months after Siegel's death, successor Gus Greenbaum was able to make the Flamingo a tremendous profit center for its owners. Greenbaum added rooms and a restaurant by Douglas Honnold, George Vernon Russell's former partner who continued to be involved in further remodelings over the next few years.

The Flamingo changed the development of Las Vegas. In plan and form, it was conceptually similar to El Rancho and the Last Frontier; stylistically it was dramatically different. By manipulating imagery, an infinite variety of new worlds could be invented. After the Flamingo, it was clear sailing in any stylistic direction.

The influence of the Flamingo was immediately felt. Beldon Katleman, owner of El Rancho Vegas, redecorated its western interior in a more sophisticated French Provincial style. "The Round-Up dining room became the Opera House, and the casino is a surprising

♠

DESERT INN, 1950, WAYNE McALLISTER, AND HUGH TAYLOR.

RUSTIC WEEPING MORTAR AND NATIVE DESERT STONE WERE COMPOSED IN A CLEAN-LINED MODERN DESIGN, HALF RANCH HOUSE, HALF NIGHTCLUB. THE SKY ROOM WAS THE TALLEST POINT IN THE CITY AT THE TIME. THE SAGUARO CACTUS FEATURED ON THE SIGN IS AN ARIZONA, NOT A NEVADA, SPECIES, "BUT IT WAS A PRETTY CACTUS," REMEMBERS ARCHITECT HUGH TAYLOR.

blend of modern and antique air," observed Paul Ralli. Katleman also added 220 rooms. Later remodelings contributed mansard roofs to the low shingled slopes.

During the late 1940s, the Las Vegas Strip gained its name. Reportedly Guy McAfee, the L.A. police captain and gambling operator, nostalgic for the rough-and-ready days of Sunset Strip gambling and nightclubbing in Los Angeles, first applied the name to the highway beyond the Las Vegas city limits. The newly opened Flamingo would have reminded McAfee of Sunset's sophisticated clubs in the 1930s. The name, with a capital S, stuck.

Las Vegas, finally realizing that it could become a major resort, followed the Flamingo with four resorts in the same image. They aimed at the same well-to-do middle-class market seeking gambling and resort relaxation. That possibility had not been obvious before; in the 1930s the city had considered limiting gambling to the downtown.

The $3 million Thunderbird opened in 1948, the same year that McCarran Airport opened an adobe-style terminal four miles south of the Flamingo as part of Las Vegas' expanding tourist strategy. In style the Thunderbird competed with the sophisticated Flamingo, but Las Vegas was not yet ready to cut all ties with its regional heritage. El Cortez builder Marion Hicks of Los Angeles had tried to expand into Reno, but then returned to Las Vegas to buy, with other investors, eleven hundred feet of Strip frontage across from the Last Frontier and El Rancho.

The Thunderbird name was derived from Native American mythology. The walls were concrete block with the ubiquitous weeping mortar, like those of El Cortez. The cocktail lounge of the Thunderbird displayed murals of cowboys, chuck wagons, and saguaro cactus; the Navajo-style dining room, named the Pow Wow Showroom, had a small stage and heavy wood trusses over the white-tablecloth-covered tables. The use of native stone connected the Thunderbird to the region. Rooms were furnished in contemporary furniture.

The Thunderbird sanded off those El Rancho motifs suited to Gene Autry movies. The broad sloping roof had the simple gable of an overgrown bunkhouse, but the lines of the columns supporting the porte cochere were crisp and modern, and the tower was unadorned

and clean. Atop it a sign marquee unctuously announced "The Thunderbird proudly presents . . ." In true ranch tradition, a white rail fence edged the leading southern edge of the property. The room wing mimicked the Flamingo's, with a central three-story section raised above the two-story wings. In front of it was the pool with high dive, palms, and lawn. It was the first Strip hotel with a covered porte cochere, a form that was later to reach remarkable heights of glitter and pretense. Perched atop the desert tower lookout above the porte cochere, its talons gripped onto the tower roof, was a cubistic neon thunderbird, in all the colors of the rainbow, a mate for the Flamingo's neon flamingo. Another neon mate perched on the roadside sign, also designed by Graham Neon. The neighboring Mobil gas station had its bright red Pegasus symbol on its sign, and El Rancho's windmill stood across the street. Together these unplanned juxtapositions of bold colors and marvelous symbols gave the Strip neighborhood a distinct aesthetic.

The Thunderbird's tower was, unlike the Flamingo's sign pylon, an integral part of the

♦

DESERT INN, 1950, WAYNE McALLISTER, AND HUGH TAYLOR. CONSTRUCTION BEGAN ON THE McALLISTER-DESIGNED MOTEL WING TO THE LEFT BEFORE OWNER WILBUR CLARK RAN OUT OF MONEY IN 1948. IT WAS EVENTUALLY REPLACED IN 1964 WITH A NINE-STORY TOWER. THE CURRENT TOWER STANDS ON THE SITE OF THE OLD CASINO AND SKY ROOM.

architecture. This sign was not propped up on a metal frame like the Golden Nugget's would be two years later downtown, but grew naturally out of the architecture. At this point in Las Vegas' development, signs did not overwhelm the architectural form; these signs were not much larger than one might find on Wilshire, Ventura, or Washington boulevards in Los Angeles. But they did reflect a natural symbiosis between sign and architecture. The Thunderbird tower presented a fanciful, colorful silhouette by night or day.

Opening in 1950, the $4.5 million, 229-room Desert Inn, "a moderately gigantic temple of chance," according to *New Yorker* writer A. J. Liebling, was an even slicker version of the Western Modern of the Thunderbird. Its creator, San Diegan Wilbur Clark, was another gambler to flee Los Angeles after reform mayor Fletcher Bowron won office in 1938. In 1944 Clark bought into El Rancho and the Monte Carlo Club on the Fremont Street site of the old Northern Club, and in 1947 the Players Club on Highway 91. Clark also had a vision, or at least a dream, of a chic resort to compete with the Flamingo, but modeled on Palm Springs, a glamorous mecca for the rich and famous.

♣

LOBBY, DESERT INN, 1950, JAC LESSMAN, INTERIOR DESIGNER. CASUAL FURNISHINGS, DESERT STONE, AND REDWOOD TRIM DEFINED THE DESERT INN'S MODERNIZED WESTERN STYLE. WINDOWS LOOKED OUT ON THE POOL.

Clark bought property across from the Last Frontier in 1945 (before the Flamingo was built) but had difficulty getting enough money in the inflationary postwar years; what had bought a resort in 1941 wouldn't in 1946. He proceeded to build piecemeal. Selecting another former San Diegan, Wayne McAllister, with whom he had worked on El Rancho remodeling, Clark clearly wanted an updated version of the Old West style. The low structures with ranch house roofs used stone and redwood. The design paralleled contemporary residential ranch houses, which borrowed the ramble if not the rusticity of actual ranch buildings.

Money ran out again when the foundations had already been built for some of the room wings. So in 1948 Clark took on Morris "Moe" Dalitz and his Ohio organization as partners. Dalitz owned several legitimate businesses, including laundries in Michigan and Ohio, which gave him connections to the Teamsters Union. In addition Dalitz also had an interest in the elegant Beverly Hills Club in Kentucky across the Ohio River from Cincinnati. Besides the floor shows and restaurant, the club had illegal gambling in upstairs rooms.

Tapped into money, Clark started again, but did not ask McAllister to continue. Dalitz was as proud of his cultivated tastes as Clark was of his, and wanted the Desert Inn to appeal to upscale gamblers. He apparently recommended an interior designer, Jac Lessman, who had worked for him before. A suave talent, Lessman was responsible for a string of hotel and resort interiors across the United States and the Caribbean. Clark's builder, Stan Harris of Los Angeles, suggested Hugh Taylor to finish the design. Taylor, age twenty-five, had been designing and drafting a number of Harris' apartment projects in West Los Angeles. He was not licensed as an architect at the time, but had apprenticed with Los Angeles architects.

During the design process Taylor and Clark traveled to different resorts Clark liked. One trip took them to Palm Springs' 1924 Desert Inn, a Spanish-style resort of low bungalows, thick adobe-style walls, and ornamented beams. Another trip took them to see the Beverly Hills Club near Cincinnati; Clark's new partners wanted Clark and his architect to see how a real casino operated. Catering to well-to-do customers, the casino had a spacious dining room and lavish shows. Clark

♥

DESERT INN, 1950, WAYNE McALLISTER, AND HUGH TAYLOR. THE PANORAMIC VIEW FROM THE THIRD-STORY SKY ROOM BAR, ITS WINDOWS SLANTED TO REDUCE REFLECTIONS, SHOWS THE TYPICALLY CASUAL RAMBLE OF THE FIRST MOTEL RESORTS. THE KACHINA DOLL RANCH, A CHILDCARE CENTER, STANDS AT THE FAR LEFT. THE MOTEL ROOMS, THE SPARKLING POOL, AND THE RUGGED MOUNTAINS CAPTURE AN ASPECT OF THE EXPERIENCE OF THE WESTERN DESERT.

♠

DESERT INN, 1950, WAYNE McALLISTER, AND HUGH TAYLOR. THE WINDOWS BELOW THE SKY ROOM WERE WILBUR CLARK'S PRIVATE OFFICE. WITH "A CARPET LIBERALLY WOVEN WITH STRANDS OF METALLIC GOLD AND SILVER, [IT] BOASTS SILVER DOLLARS AS KNOBS FOR ITS VARIOUS DESKS, DRAWERS AND FILING CABINETS," REPORTED LUCIUS BEEBE IN HOLIDAY MAGAZINE. PUBLICITY PHOTOS LIKE THIS WOULD BE DISTRIBUTED TO NORTHERN PAPERS IN MIDWINTER TO TEMPT VISITORS TO LAS VEGAS.

and Dalitz wanted the same tone in the Desert Inn. The difference, of course, was that the gambling could be public in Las Vegas, not hidden upstairs with doors to block it off in case of a police raid. Bringing the casino out of the back room made a difference to the design. In Kentucky dealers wore garters and eyeshades under subdued light. The Desert Inn casino had excellent lighting and dealers wore white shirts. The Desert Inn's showroom was larger and more professional than the Beverly Hills Club's. These and other elements evolved into a new formula in Las Vegas.

With Clark closely involved, Taylor and Lessman finished the main casino building, enlarging and rearranging the McAllister plan as Clark and his new partners had new ideas. Returning from a trip to San Francisco that included a visit to the Mark Hopkins Hotel's urbane Top of the Mark lounge designed in 1936 by Timothy Pflueger, Clark wanted a Las Vegas version and asked Taylor if he could include a similar vista point. Taylor designed the Sky Room atop the three-story

stair tower that dominated the street facade. "Glass enclosed on three sides, this lounge is reminiscent of an airport lookout tower. The surrounding desert, mountains, and far reaching tropically landscaped grounds are clearly visible at all times. At night tiny electric stars twinkling in the ceiling of the lounge make it seem one with the surrounding desert," reported *Architect and Engineer*. It claimed to be the tallest building in town.

The Desert Inn appeared along the Strip as a large sloping roof accented by the three-story tower. A circular drive led to the entry, a broad porch lined with ashlar pillars and lounge chairs. A fountain spraying water sixty feet high stood in the middle of the lawn ringed by the drive, providing a balance to the pool across the street at the Last Frontier. A sidewalk connected the two casinos. Trees planted within the circular drive created an almost parklike setting. The $4.5 million hotel was Bermuda pink with green trim. One- and two-story room wings interspersed with parking lots ringed the pool patio behind the main building on the seventeen-acre site. Taylor says he "never considered the Desert Inn a motel per se because of its luxurious appointments, but really eighty to ninety percent of the clientele came by car." He had to allow for visibility as they rode down the Strip, "and the convenience to have a place to park the car reasonably close to the room. But this was meant as a place for people to stay awhile."

The cinder block structure was trimmed with a sandstone veneer quarried in Arizona and Nevada. Weeping mortar brick faced the stair tower. Redwood was used throughout the interior, including the lobby registration desk and ceiling trim. The large roof was concrete shakes. The floor was flagstone. Like other resorts, the entire hotel was air-conditioned, already common in Las Vegas. The use of native stone and redwood, of clean, abstract lines, wide eaves, and porches, was influenced, says Taylor, by the architecture of Frank Lloyd Wright in Arizona.

Entering through the shady porch, visitors turned left to reach the hotel registry. To the right was the eighty-by-sixty-foot windowless casino. A rawhide bar decorated with stylized steer heads and raw leather straps dominated the Celebrity Room bar. A drugstore with soda fountain, dress shops, beauty salon, radio station, apparel shops, curio shops, and a barber shop made the hotel a small town. "A tremendous wood-burning fireplace, set corner wise, adds warmth, but in no way interrupts the view of the center patio and landscaped gardens through one entire glassed-in wall," reported *Architect and Engineer*. Beyond the casino lay the coffee shop; the dining room, which overlooked the pool; the 450-seat Painted Desert showroom with hand-painted murals featuring abstract western motifs; and the kitchen. This wing hooked around the turquoise blue, figure-eight pool in the center of the site, ringed by a half circle of one-story motel rooms. Cabanas edged the pool. At the north end of the pool was the Kachina Doll Ranch, an early attempt to cultivate the family tourist trade. The ranch was a childcare center with playroom/cribroom, staffed by a trained psychologist. Beyond the room wings lay the open desert, crossed by the native flora of ground-hugging asphalt roads and leafless telephone poles.

Like the Thunderbird, the Desert Inn also had a tower capped with a sign, the Desert Inn's palette-shaped logo with rustic and script lettering scrawling "Wilbur Clark's Desert Inn" across it. The sheet metal sign by the Young Electric Sign Company (YESCO) grew integrally out of the brick tower. It was a brilliant bit of roadside ornament. The cloud shape, a feature of the desert landscape, was captured in tactile sheet metal, and poised with perfect artificiality against the real clouds and real desert. At night it was outlined in neon lightning. The palette shape was a roadside version of the free forms seen in modern art (Miró, Calder, and others) and architecture of the period. As at the Thunderbird, sign and architecture were in balance. There was no need to grab attention with large signs, as there would be later when competition grew and the Strip filled in with more hotels. Clark, a skilled promoter, tied the sign imagery in with matchbooks, menus, and other souvenirs.

The five Strip resorts offered "an assembly of glittering chrome and flaming colors by day, a flowering jungle of glowing neon and flashing lights by night," wrote *New York Times* reporter Gladwin Hill in 1951, comparing it to a "Broadway-in-the-Sagebrush" for his East Coast readers. The luxury of the Desert Inn set standards the other resorts

CLUB BINGO, LOS ANGELES HIGHWAY, C. 1948. LOCATED ACROSS THE HIGHWAY FROM EL RANCHO VEGAS, CLUB BINGO WAS A CASINO, NOT A HOTEL. IT MIXED STYLES: THE BONANZA ROOM SHOWED FREMONT STREET'S OLD WEST INFLUENCE WHILE THE STRIKING MODERNE PYLON WAS DESIGNED FOR THE STRIP.

♣

scrambled to meet over the next few years. When the Desert Inn opened its large pool, the Last Frontier across the highway filled in its old roadside pool and "built a heated one of AAU dimensions with a subsurface observation room at the deep end and a deck-side bar," wrote Dick Pearce in *Harper's* in 1955. The Desert Inn then replaced its original pool with one even bigger, only to have the Sands create "a thing of free flow design large enough to float a cruiser." The Tropicana countered with underwater Muzak.

While reporting on these spectacles, the press wondered, as did many Las Vegans, when the bubble would burst. Many worried when Senator Estes Kefauver brought his organized crime hearings to Las Vegas in 1950. His spotlight on gambling nationwide, however, may have been a boon for Las Vegas: the heat closed down the competition in other states and sent many gamblers scurrying to the one legal haven.

Las Vegas looked prosperous enough. "The lush Las Vegan resorts are scattered along the highway leading from the airport into town, a distance of eight miles. This is known as the Strip. There are five major hotel-casinos on the Strip . . . and a couple, like the Bingo Club, that from the road look hardly smaller. All are made up of wide-flung low buildings centering on great outdoor swimming pools, and all are surrounded by the vivid green that lavish employment of artesian-well water can produce in the desert. Some desolate, Tunisian-looking mountains, the Charleston Range, stand off to one side, and in the interstices between the great hotels there are motels, pizza joints, and wedding chapels," reported *The New Yorker's* A. J. Liebling in 1950.

The Bingo Club, a Strip casino since 1947, became the seed for the next resort, the $2 million Sahara, opening in 1952 across from El Rancho Vegas. Milton Prell, a jeweler from Los Angeles, was the active partner in building the Sahara, though contractor Del Webb took part of his pay in a partnership. The architect was Max Meltzmann, who had been working in Los Angeles since the 1920s. Architecturally it followed the basic pattern of the Desert Inn and the Thunderbird. It featured a tall brick pylon at the entry anchoring low wings that

♥

BELOW (LEFT): **SAHARA, 1952, MAX MELTZMANN.** THE CONGO ROOM DURING A REHEARSAL. MURALS OF AFRICAN WARRIORS WERE THE ONLY TOUCHES THAT BROUGHT THIS ROOM ANYWHERE NEAR AFRICA. BUT THE PROSCENIUM'S AKIMBO ANGLES AND THE FLOATING CEILING SOFFIT (WITH REFLECTED LIGHT) MADE IT BRIGHTLY MODERN.

BELOW (RIGHT): **SAHARA, 1952, MAX MELTZMANN.** THE ORIGINAL QUADRANGLE PROTECTED THE POOL. LATER MOTEL WINGS TO THE SOUTH (RIGHT), ADDED IN 1953, WERE THE FIRST LAS VEGAS PROJECT BY ARCHITECT MARTIN STERN, JR. IN THE FOREGROUND CAN BE SEEN SOME EL RANCHO BUNGALOWS.

spun outward from its center like a pinwheel. The tower's height was justified by the sign on top of it. The motif was similar to the 1926 Arizona Biltmore in Phoenix by Frank Lloyd Wright, where the sculptural elements of the textile block provided ornament; for the roadside hotel, signage became the ornament.

The Sahara's theme was North African; plaster statues of camels and Arabs lounging outside and the Congo Room inside welcomed guests. The Casbah Lounge and Caravan Room, looking over the pool terrace, completed the theming. Like the other recent hotels, the Sahara was a motel in form. A low main building with lobby and casino stood at the front; to the rear, the glassy restaurants looked out on a manicured lawn ringed by two-story motel units (206 rooms in all) with balconies or patios. Lucius Beebe exclaimed about its "twenty acres of landscaped ground with rare blossoms and shrubs to make even Boston's Public Gardens look to its tulips."

The 1952 Sands brought the talented eclectic, Wayne McAllister, back to Las Vegas once again. Instead of El Rancho's western splendors, this time he brought the popular late Moderne style from Los Angeles, where he and partner William Wagner were perfecting the style in restaurant designs, including the popular Bob's Big Boy chain and the upscale Lawry's on La Cienega's Restaurant Row. Unlike the case of Wilbur Clark, the Sands' owners did not become involved in the design. McAllister had a free

hand. The result was the most elegant piece of architecture the Strip had seen.

Technically the Sands was a remodel of the Club LaRue, a stylish French restaurant opened by Los Angeles gambler Billy Wilkerson in 1950. The existing structure built on the sidewalk dictated the Sands' location close to the highway, though McAllister would have preferred a setback to allow for easier car access. The view from approaching cars shaped the design as it had in the earlier hotels, but the Sands was even more dramatic and modern.

The casino, basically a warehouse for gaming, was flat-roofed. McAllister's deft placement of an eye-catching porte cochere and a zigzag wall ornamented with tiled planters along the sidewalk subdued the cavernous mass of the structure. The Sands' porte cochere went far beyond the Thunderbird's to become striking

ABOVE: **SANDS HOTEL, 1952, WAYNE MCALLISTER.**

BELOW: **SANDS, 1952, WAYNE MCALLISTER.** THE SANDS CASINO WAS NOT ILLUMINATED AS BRIGHTLY AS THE SAHARA'S. LIGHT FOCUSED ATTENTION AT THE PERIPHERY WHERE VISITORS COULD FIND THE BAR, RESTAURANTS, AND COPA ROOM.

"The main building of the Sands is a great rectangular hall, with the reception desk in one corner, slot machines along one long wall, and a bar and cocktail lounge, complete with Latin trio, along the wall opposite. In the middle is a jumble of roulette and craps tables and twenty-one layouts," reported *The New Yorker's* A. J. Liebling in 1953. Three wide terrazzo stairs led down into the large low casino lit by shallow modern chandeliers. Around the periphery, marquees marked the entry to the Copa Room and the restaurants; separated by columns from the main room was a bar featuring a stylized bas-relief mural of galloping wagons, buttes, Joshua trees, and cowboys. Overhead skylights illuminated the Garden Room restaurant.

Crowning the Sands was a roadside sign that took a first step beyond the Strip status quo of sheet metal signs adorned with neon. At fifty-six feet, it was taller than the rest (the *S* alone was thirty-five feet), but its primary distinction was its integration into the main building's architecture. McAllister designed this slender and elegant sign, repeating motifs from the building itself; YESCO fabricated it. This sign was more a piece of architecture than a sign on a post. An eggcrate grill, cantilevered from a solid anchor pylon, played with desert light and shadow. In a bold free script, the neon name "Sands" sprawled across the face of the contrasting rigorous grid. It was not a signboard but an architectonic piece. A secondary sign stood by the southern highway turn-in. Later an attraction board listing headliners' names was added beneath the name "Sands" of the main sign. This sign set off a scramble by the other hotels to keep up in size, eye appeal, and stylistic sophistication.

"The five postwar hotels have that rich sleekness of modern design that suggests suavity and impermanence. Soft colors, soft lights, and the cool dimness so blessed on the desert. Dewy lawns laid on imported soil, and painfully maintained against nature. Handsome, yes; inviting, yes. But little incongruities keep alerting you to where you are," wrote journalist Dick Pearce in *Harper's* in 1955.

modern sculpture. Three sharp-edged beams jutted out from the roof over the glass-walled entry and then angled down into the earth as fins. A horizontal plane dotted with can lights and suspended from the beams sheltered arriving gamblers. Two chrome-clad frames, a late Moderne motif, featured coming attractions. The two-story glass entry was bordered by a wall of marble. Along the circular drive, an extraordinary line of sculptural metal columns and stuccoed pylons containing integral lighting created a screen between the entry and the pool gardens. Four two-story motel wings, each with fifty rooms, stretched back on the lot.

Among the incongruities were acts booked in hell, like the 1954 pairing of Robert Merrill and Louis Armstrong at the Sands. With an aggressive entertainment policy, the Sands had a reputation as "New York's Copacabana Gone West," which fed the town's growing popularity as an entertainment capital. In the 1950s astronomical amounts were spent luring top-name entertainers as headliners: Frank Sinatra, Marlene Dietrich, Lena Horne, even Noel Coward. Hotels justified the salaries because big names lured customers into the casinos, where the real profit was turned. Las Vegas' warped pay scales aided the demise of nightclubs across the nation which, lacking the gambling subsidy, couldn't afford to compete for headliners. Even the biggest clubs in New York, Chicago, and Los Angeles could not afford the record-breaking $50,000 per week the Riviera paid Liberace in 1955.

Competition from the ultramodern Sands compelled the Flamingo to remodel in 1953. Only six years old, it looked dated in the accelerating rush of new hotels. While the casino remained open, the interior was redecorated with cork, brass, and iron circles in a style the *Las Vegas Sun* identified as "Aztec-modern." "Nightmare-shaped pieces

of driftwood are installed in planters bordering windows which overlook the swimming pool," continued the paper. The Flamingo's original entry and signs were torn down, and a long facade and porch capped with an upswept roof were built. The "Flamingo" name floated above the fascia. The facade was green quartzite quarried in Oregon. At one end stood a sixty-foot-tall cylindrical sign covered with animated neon circles that blinked on and off in an upward motion like champagne bubbles effervescing into the air. A new roadside sign echoed the theme. Pereira and Luckman of Los Angeles was the architect; YESCO designed the sign. This and other new signs formed "a palpitating sea of electric illumination," reported the *New York Times*' Gladwin Hill in 1953. There were now eighteen hundred hotel rooms on the Strip and the average stay was three days. A first-class hotel charged $7.50 per day; a motel, $3.00.

"All seven pleasure domes have a conventionalized layout—an imposing lobby; beyond it a spacious lounge-bar; beyond that the casino proper; and, significantly, beyond that the lavish restaurant-night clubs which are the showcases for the parade of big-name entertainers," con-

♣

FLAMINGO, 1953, PEREIRA AND LUCKMAN. MEMORIES OF THE ORIGINAL FLAMINGO WERE SWEPT AWAY BY THE DAZZLING 1953 REMODEL, OFTEN MISTAKENLY REFERRED TO AS THE ORIGINAL. IT STRETCHED A MODERNISTIC COLONNADE OF GLOWING COLUMNS ALL THE WAY TO THE STRIP, WHERE A TOWER OF NEON RINGS BUBBLED LIGHT INTO THE DESERT SKY. BEYOND IT CAN BE SEEN THE DUNES' SULTAN ASTRIDE HIS PORTE COCHERE.

LEFT: **FLAMINGO, C. 1966, PEREIRA AND LUCKMAN.** A STUDY OF THE FLAMINGO'S ROOF REVEALS THE ACCRETION OF ADDITIONS OVER THE YEARS. THE T-SHAPED ROOM WINGS ON THE LEFT BEYOND THE ORIGINAL HOTEL WERE ADDED IN 1955 BY LOS ANGELES ARCHITECT DOUGLAS HONNOLD. THE RESIDENTIAL AND COMMERCIAL DEVELOPMENT TO THE EAST OF THE STRIP CAN ALSO BE SEEN AT THE TOP OF THIS PHOTO.

RIGHT: **FLAMINGO LOUNGE, 1953, PEREIRA AND LUCKMAN.**

tinued Hill. "They are elaborately furnished salons bathed in eerie artificial light. . . . Thick carpets and acoustic paneling muffle the welter of sounds into a low-key chorus— murmurs of elation, sighs of despair, the clanking thud of slot machines, the unending drone of the stickmen."

When the Last Frontier remodeled in 1955, it also added a new sign, a 126-foot tri-sided pylon of stacked cones lit indirectly. The attraction board was at eye level. The Thunderbird's family of neon birds remained perched on tower and roadside signs but the roadside bird was lifted higher into the air on a pylon rising out of a new porte cochere. The Desert Inn brought its western Modernism up to the roadside with an arch, a wooden bent resting on a

♠

NEW FRONTIER, 1955. COMPETING WITH THE ELEGANT NEW SANDS AND THE FLAMINGO'S CHAMPAGNE TOWER, THE LAST FRONTIER'S WESTERNISMS GAVE WAY TO THE NEW FRONTIER'S MODERNISMS. FRAGMENTS OF THE OLD RANCH-STYLE LAST FRONTIER COULD STILL BE GLIMPSED ON THE OTHER SIDE OF THE NEW FRONTIER'S CLEAN LINES AND DECORATIVE SCREENS, BUT BY THE EARLY 1960s THEY WOULD DEGENERATE, WITH ONLY MEMORIES OF THE OLD ROADSIDE POOL AMBIENCE REMAINING.

pylon of native stone. In addition, throughout the mid-1950s almost every hotel added lowrise room wings, incipient convention centers, and bigger casinos in the rush to keep up.

Such bold sign forms scattered along the Strip made a distinctive landscape of symbols and lights. The bigger signs were efforts to visually bridge the distance between highway and hotel as Strip designers experimented with forms and techniques that worked in the Strip's broad landscape. The hotels were still recognizably architectural. Views glimpsed across the intervening parking lots were of ranch houses and nightclubs.

The Last Frontier, bastion of high westernism, followed the Flamingo with a 1955 restyling. In 1951 William Moore had sold the Last Frontier to Guy McAfee associate Jacob Kozloff and Beldon Katleman of El Rancho Vegas. Changing the name to the New Frontier (a name Jack Kennedy could not have helped seeing when he visited the nearby Sands in the late 1950s), the new owners abandoned the Old West theme for a sleek modern look more in keeping with the contemporary General Motors Technical Center in Warren, Michigan, by Eero Saarinen than with any dude ranch. Built just north of the still-standing older hotel, it echoed the two-story scale and second-story balconies of the old. A crisp porte cochere with an upswept lip and "New Frontier" in large block letters sheltered arriving Cadillacs. The original buildings remained for a few more years but the gracious highway frontage with pool and lawn was replaced with parking. The irregular facade was joined under one long roof accented by a large sign scaled up for the new age.

Inside, the modern theme was carried out in exuberant space-age motifs not too different from the quasi-spaceship ornamental elements of Saarinen's honored GM Tech Center (or Disney's Tomorrowland, opening the same year). The Cloud 9 cocktail lounge had relief murals of celestial objects; planets were featured in the dining room; the Venus

◆

TOP: **DESERT INN, c. 1956, WAYNE McALLISTER, HUGH TAYLOR.** TO GAIN A FOOTHOLD ON THE HIGHWAY, THE DESERT INN ADDED WOOD AND STONE ARCHES. WITH SUCCESS, THE SKY ROOM WAS EXPANDED BY WRAPPING IT AROUND THE TOWER.

MIDDLE: **DUNES, 1955, ROBERT DORR, JR., AND JOHN REPLOGLE.** THE FIBERGLASS SULTAN BROUGHT THE GIGANTISM OF FREMONT STREET'S 1951 VEGAS VIC OUT TO THE STRIP. MOVED FROM THE ROOF OF THE DUNES TO THE REAR OF THE DUNES PROPERTY IN 1964, THIS ROADSIDE STATUE OVERLOOKED INTERSTATE 15 UNTIL THE SULTAN BURNED IN THE LATE 1980S.

BOTTOM: **RIVIERA, 1955, ROY FRANCE AND SON.** MIAMI MODERN OFFICIALLY ARRIVED IN LAS VEGAS WITH THE NINE-STORY RIVIERA, BACKED BY MIAMI MONEY AND CONSTRUCTED BY A MIAMI BUILDER.

dinner theater's stage revolved like the solar system. The color scheme was a bit brighter than would be found in high-art versions like Saarinen's: Italian marble floors and pink-and-white leather sofas, lilac carpeting in the casino, and violet and magenta walls. Chandeliers took the form of flying saucers and spinning planets. The Thunderbird also expanded its casino out toward the road, framing its new second floor with a rectangular box. A new porte cochere and a taller sign pole with three pennant signboards attached were added.

But when the Dunes, the Royal Nevada, and the Riviera all opened in 1955, many feared that Las Vegas had stretched too far. The city was only beginning to update its infrastructure to handle growth; Lake Mead water, for example, would arrive in September 1955 to supplement the wells on which earlier hotels had depended. The $10 million Riviera, built in 1955 next to the Thunderbird, was the Strip's first highrise, a record-breaking nine stories with 291 rooms, a departure from the Strip's motel format. Many had doubted the desert soil could support something that tall. It had the earmarks of a Miami hotel, and indeed its backers and its architect, Roy France and Son, were based in Miami; France had designed the streamlined 1939 Sands Hotel in Miami Beach, as well as apartments. J. Maher Weller of Las Vegas was the Riviera's associate architect. A block with banks of horizontal strip windows marked the center of the tower block, with framed wraparound windows delineating the corners. A contrasting nine-story elevator tower festooned with decorative gold buttons put it in the Miami camp. Inside, fleur-de-lis wallpaper

♣

ROYAL NEVADA, 1955, PAUL WILLIAMS AND JOHN REPLOGLE. THE PYLON FRONTED A FOUNTAIN OF NEON TUBING. THOUGH SEVERAL HOTELS STRUGGLED FINANCIALLY IN THE MID-1950S, THE ROYAL NEVADA WAS THE ONLY ONE TO DISAPPEAR COMPLETELY, SWALLOWED IN 1959 BY THE STARDUST.

MOULIN ROUGE, 1955. THOUGH FAR FROM THE STRIP ON WEST BONANZA ROAD, THE MOULIN ROUGE BORROWED THE STRIP STYLE. IT IS AN EXCELLENT EXAMPLE OF THE USE OF SCALE (IN THE SCRIPT FASCIA SIGN), MULTIDIRECTIONAL FACES (ON THE PYLON), AND THE MODERNIST COMPOSITION OF LARGE-SCALE PATTERNS AND VARIED BLOCKS TO BRING COHESION TO A BUILDING ON A LARGE STRIP SITE.

HACIENDA HOTEL, 1956. THE SINGLE STRONG FORMAL GESTURE OF THE HACIENDA'S CURVED FACADE STOOD OUT IN THE RELATIVE EMPTINESS OF THE MID-1950S STRIP. LOCATED A MILE AND A HALF SOUTH OF THE FLAMINGO, THE HACIENDA, PART OF A CALIFORNIA MOTEL CHAIN, WAS CLOSE TO MCCARRAN AIRPORT AND HAD ITS OWN FLEET OF PLANES TO FLY IN GAMBLERS FROM ALL OVER THE COUNTRY.

FREMONT AND SECOND STREETS, c. 1952. THESE TWO PICTURES ILLUSTRATE THE GROWING IMPACT OF LARGE-SCALE NEON SIGNS IN CREATING AN URBAN SPACE.

mirrored the French Provincial style of Miami's Fontainebleau. A pylon sign skewered the thin porte cochere like a toothpick through a cheese canapé; a second V-shaped marquee sign stood at the roadside entry.

The Dunes and the Royal Nevada were both in the lowrise motel tradition. The Dunes featured a porte cochere both modern and nomadic, with sloping stucco walls that echoed desert tents. Astride its roof stood a thirty-five-foot-tall fiberglass sultan with billowing cape and plumed turban created by YESCO. He joined the Pioneer Club's waving cowboy on Fremont Street, both part of the rich roadside tradition of giant oranges, hot dogs, hats, and people used as three-dimensional signs. The $3.5 million Dunes stood catercorner to the Flamingo and was the hotel farthest south on the Strip. It had two hundred rooms on 85 acres and a ninety-foot pool. A golf course was added in 1959, reflecting the fact that men were the resorts' target market. The design was by Robert Dorr, Jr., of Hollywood's Warner Agency, with architect/engineer John Replogle.

The Royal Nevada, north of the New Frontier, brought to Las Vegas another Los Angeles architect of note, Paul Williams working with John Replogle. Like the offices of George Vernon Russell and Douglas Honnold, Williams' practice in the 1930s and 1940s mixed a suave Hollywood Modernism with solid historical revivalism. The Royal Nevada featured a curving entry canopy and a large fountainlike sculpture of neon.

Also opening in 1955 was the Moulin Rouge, Las Vegas' first integrated casino. Significantly it was on West Bonanza Road, well off the Strip. Las Vegas was notoriously racist; blacks were segregated on the poor west side of town and only hired on the Strip as maids and busboys. Even headliners like Lena Horne, Billy Eckstine, and the Will Mastin Trio with Sammy Davis, Jr., were rarely allowed to stay at the hotels at which they were performing. Blacks had their own clubs (the Harlem Club, the Brown Derby) on the west side. The Moulin Rouge was reminiscent of

♥

GOLDEN NUGGET, 1946. DURING THE WAR, DOWNTOWN PROMOTERS DECIDED TO STRENGTHEN THEIR COLLECTIVE IMAGE BY ADOPTING OLD WEST IMAGERY. THE GOLDEN NUGGET, THE MOST THOROUGH RESULT OF THAT PLAN, CREATED ITS VERSION OF A BARBARY COAST SALOON. THE SKELETON SIGN OVERHEAD WAS ADDED IN 1950.

♠

BOULDER CLUB, 1946.
THIS VERTICAL SIGN IN-
TRODUCED THE YOUNG
ELECTRIC SIGN COMPANY
TO LAS VEGAS.

Rancho Vegas, one of a California chain of motels in Fresno, Bakersfield, and Indio. But Las Vegas was in trouble. After the failure of the Royal Nevada and serious problems in keeping the Dunes and Riviera open, the Strip clearly needed new markets to exploit if it was to grow. Other states threatened to legalize gambling. Unlike Phoenix and Albuquerque which had industry, Las Vegas was dependent on tourism. The Hacienda began by appealing to the family market with several pools and a go-cart track and no showroom or expensive restaurants. It was known by professional gamblers as "Hayseed Heaven" because of its local ownership, but it managed to survive with a fleet of planes bringing gamblers from Los Angeles, San Francisco, Chicago, St. Louis, Detroit, and New York.

The city's sybaritic image led to public criticism typified by that of Julian Halevy in *The Nation* in 1958: Las Vegas "narcotizes the number-one preoccupation of daily reality . . . the Almighty Buck. . . . a luxury world where the fact of money seems beneath notice; a world of Olympic swimming pools, hanging gardens, waitresses beautiful as movie stars, marble baths and bars a block long, air conditioning, deep carpets, royal buffets and obsequious waiters offering free drinks. The illusion is created that we are all rich, that money means nothing."

Las Vegas' architectural evolution relied on unexpected jumps. El Rancho Vegas had taken Las Vegas in a new direction by colonizing the Strip; then the Flamingo's sophistication opened a new theme that inspired most of the growth in the early 1950s. Innovations in signage and services on downtown Fremont Street would soon show up on the suburban Strip, and vice versa.

The sophistication of the Flamingo, Desert Inn, and Sands did not affect Fremont Street, which still gloried in its Old West style. In 1946 the Chamber of Commerce named three blocks of Fremont Street "Glitter Gulch," thereby fusing the modern sheen and the Old West theme. The style's popularity was felt statewide. Harvey Gross opened the Wagon Wheel Saloon at Lake Tahoe in 1946, and Harolds Club in Reno featured a facade mural of the Old West as wide as the building itself. Fremont felt little pressure to respond to the new Strip resorts in the late 1940s; the Strip had largely created its own market and brought in new customers. Many Strip

the Sands, with a tall billboard pylon. Though it had difficulties maintaining its integrated policy, it remained opened until the early 1960s, when the Strip began integrating in the face of civil rights demonstrations by local blacks. Positive publicity was the lifeblood of the town's tourist industry, and hotel owners wanted to avoid controversy at all costs.

The 266-room Hacienda, opened in 1955, was, like El

and downtown establishments had the same owners.

The Golden Nugget, opened in 1946, set a standard for Fremont Street as the Flamingo would for the Strip later in the year. Investors, including Guy McAfee, created a dazzling new casino out of a nondescript two-story commercial block at the corner of Second and Fremont. It chose the western vernacular of urban Gold Rush San Francisco, the Barbary Coast style, and the suitable signs were designed by YESCO's Dick Porter.

Evoking not Nevada but California precedents, it supposedly echoed the opulent gambling dens that lined San Francisco's nineteenth century red-light district. The facade was painted in rococo curlicues. In 1950 a large sign was added, lifted clear of the roof on a steel framework one hundred feet in the air. Designed by YESCO's Hermon Boernge, it was a radiant phantasm of neon and incandescent light that emblazoned Gilded Age gingerbread and a scintillating nugget against the sky. It set off another round of bigger and brighter signs on Fremont Street.

Of course there is no precedent in the architecture of the Gilded Age for such a sign. The rest of the exterior was likewise fanciful; Gold Rush casinos such as San Francisco's plush El Dorado of the 1850s were stone; the saloons of the rowdier, cruder Barbary Coast, typically unadorned brick. Inside, however, the Golden Nugget did model the atmosphere of that well-documented era. The El Dorado's main gambling room was well lit with gas globe chandeliers hung from a high ceiling supported by slender columns. Heavy curtains hung from the windows, paintings of nudes furnished the room, and an ornate carved wood bar with mirror behind it stretched along one wall. "They look more like palaces than gambling dens," wrote French journalist Etienne Derbec of these casinos. Like the Las Vegas casinos that were yet to come, it "seduced" visitors "in a measure [that] he loses his senses" wrote a German traveler in 1856.

The Golden Nugget had paintings of nudes on the walls, above the bar, and on top of the slot machines. Carved wood ornament and furniture filled the lounge and the ceiling was held up by two carved unclothed females with two carved satyrs nearby. "The Nugget glitters splendidly with floriated electroliers, Turkey carpets, plush, ormolu and cloisonné and some of the most amazing nudes on record,"

reported Lucius Beebe in *Holiday*.

The patina of Old West sinfulness and western history identifies the Golden Nugget as theme architecture, a history that never was. The "1905" inscription on the corner confused the issue even more, being the date of Las Vegas' founding, not of the gambling hall's. But these historical

PIONEER CLUB, 1951.
THE SCALE OF LETTERING AND SIGNS HAD BEEN INCREASING STEADILY SINCE 1940. NOW A SIXTY-FOOT COWBOY NAMED VEGAS VIC EXPLODED THE SCALE OF IMAGERY ON FREMONT STREET AS WELL.

♣

ABOVE: **FREMONT STREET, C. 1946.**

BELOW: **HORSESHOE CLUB, C. 1953.** BEFORE THE GROUND FLOOR OF THE HOTEL APACHE WAS RENAMED THE HORSESHOE, THE ELDORADO CLUB HAD REMODELED IT WITH SLEEK CHROME DISPLAY WINDOWS, ASHLAR VENEER, OVERHEAD MARQUEE, AND PLATE GLASS TO PUT THE SLOT MACHINES AND THE ACTION ON DISPLAY.

marquee angled like a theater's. This sign introduced the fabled Young Electric Sign Company, of Salt Lake City, to Las Vegas. Circular blades trimmed the leading edge of the forty-foot sign. Plate glass shaded by venetian blinds opened the first floor to full view of the street.

The Pioneer Club adapted by adding neon wagons, western vistas, and cactus to its sidewalk canopy. But its major contribution to the sign wars was Vegas Vic. In 1945 the Chamber of Commerce had started the Live Wire Fund, a booster organization supported by casino contributions, to promote Las Vegas as a tourist destination. With these funds they hired the J. Walter Thompson advertising agency to market the city. Ads soon de-emphasized western splendor in favor of the desert paradise getaway. In 1947 the West-Marquis agency replaced Thompson and reintroduced the western theme with one of the most popular icons of the Las Vegas hagiography, Vegas Vic. The lanky cowboy with cigarette in mouth and a ready "Howdy Pardner" appeared in ads, brochures, and billboards throughout the West.

Vegas Vic first appeared for the Pioneer Club in the late 1940s on a steel frame sign atop a 1910 brick building across the street from the club on the corner of First and Fremont. His neon thumb wagged toward the establishment across the street. "Here it is! The famous Pioneer Club," said the sign in three type styles: a movie-trailer paintbrush-swipe type, a fluid script denoting quiet assurance, and a bluff, rustic nailed-stick style. In 1951 he stepped across the street, now in full figure, sixty feet tall, animated, and towering above the roof. Outlined in tubing, the cowboy's neon cigarette dangled as his recorded voice spoke to sidewalk customers, and his sheet metal arm, hand, and thumb gestured to the club. Figurative gigantism added another tool to Fremont sign designers' bag of tricks and later influenced the Dunes' sultan. YESCO fabricated him, as well as twins in Wendover and Laughlin, Nevada, in later years.

discrepancies had little impact on the quality of the architecture. The Golden Nugget set a standard that remained Fremont Street's favored motif for a decade.

In 1946 Las Vegas' Eldorado Club had taken over the ground floor of the Hotel Apache from the New Western Casino (which had taken over from a jewelry store). It also claimed that its sign, featuring a miner striking gold at the corner of the marquee beside the name, was "the largest electric sign west of the Mississippi River." The same year the Boulder Club switched over to a larger, streamlined sign over a

Like much of Fremont Street, the Pioneer Club was a gambling bazaar. The casino opened to the sidewalk with glass walls that slid back, glass windows, and swinging doors. The underside of the sidewalk canopy was laced with neon tubing to extend the domain of the casino into the public realm. It was an urban variation on the residential architectural concept of blurring inside and out.

In 1948 Steve Hannegan and Associates replaced West-Marquis after successfully promoting Sun Valley, Idaho, as a resort for the Union Pacific railroad. Their major contribution was founding the Desert Sea News Bureau (later renamed the Las Vegas News Bureau) which documented the city with extraordinary thoroughness. Their forte was bathing beauties and stars posed strategically by a hotel's pool so that the hotel's name was visible in the picture reprinted in midwinter in newspapers nationwide. They also created the most thorough documentation of the Las Vegas architectural phenomenon available, due to the city's rapid rate of remodeling. Through the 1940s and into the 1950s, the city promoted itself as the gateway to a western wonderland of ready hospitality and scenes of desert splendor—in a city that also happened to have gambling. By the 1950s, Las Vegas was promoting itself as a glamorous gambling city, and Lake Mead boating and Hoover Dam were sidelights.

In 1949, before Vegas Vic appeared on the Pioneer Club in 1951, the Las Vegas Club moved across the street and erected a 120-foot Moderne sign designed by YESCO's Hermon Boernge. It was taller than the Boulder Club's, with huge, upright Old West typeface letters marching along the canopy marquee. Neon coins spilled from a giant slot machine at its base. By the early 1960s the Las Vegas Club had swallowed the neighboring Overland Hotel with a continuous marquee where several smaller storefronts once stood. "Biff's Famous Food" perched alongside "Las Vegas Club" on the marquee. The scale of the letters overwhelmed the still-visible

♣

LAS VEGAS CLUB, C. 1960. MOVING TO THE NORTH SIDE OF FREMONT IN 1949, THE LAS VEGAS CLUB JOINED THE RACE TO INCREASE THE SCALE OF SIGNAGE BY OVERWHELMING ITS TWO-STORY BUILDING WITH LETTERS EIGHT FEET TALL. LIGHTS INSIDE THE LETTERS FLASHED. TOWERING OVER THE NEIGHBORING NEON, ITS NEW BLADE SIGN TOPPED THE PIONEER AND THE BOULDER CLUBS' IN SLENDERNESS AND DARING; YESCO'S HERMON BOERNGE WAS THE DESIGNER.

building and windows behind, establishing an entirely different scale to the street. In the early 1960s a slot machine the size of a building joined it next door.

In a fluid script reserved for Roadmasters, the "Eldorado Club" became the "Horseshoe" gambling saloon in 1950, run by Texas gambler Benny Binion, and fronted by Joe W. Brown while Binion was serving a prison term in his homestate in the early 1950s. A horseshoe and horse replaced the corner miner. The 1950 Westerner next to the Pioneer

Club offered a different approach to signage. Instead of using neon, it returned to the classic billboard, devoting its full facade to an illuminated panorama of desert buttes and pioneers. The atmosphere of these clubs was infused with the hard surfaces of chrome and plate glass, and the glare and glow of neon on overhead canopies that eliminated shadows.

As the sign race accelerated, they moved from pictorial Indian chief heads, overland trains, and ornamental details into larger and larger patterns covering the entire faces of buildings. From there it was an easy step for the signs to evolve architectural volume and presence. Some were abstract, others marvelously fanciful three-dimensional versions of Victorian bric-a-brac. Just as Detroit car designers in the same period explored the design possibilities of sheet metal and glass technology, sign artists explored the urban impact and beauty of their medium. These

fantasies of Fremont Street directly influenced such neon landmarks as the Flamingo's 1953 champagne tower.

The density of imagery and light encrusting the three blocks of Fremont made it a place without equal. Silhouetted against the sky, glowing symbols balanced on top of overhangs, marking corners with singular shapes. During 1955, Fremont Street offered the curious prospect of slender neon towers (the Boulder, the Las Vegas Club) reaching skyward, joined by heraldic patches branded on the sky (the Golden Nugget, the Hotel Apache), giants (the Pioneer

♥

THE WESTERNER, 1950. INSTEAD OF FEATURING A SINGLE VANE SIGN HUNG OUTSIDE, THE WESTERNER TURNED ITS ENTIRE FACADE INTO A BILLBOARD SIGN DEPICTING THE BUTTES AND PIONEERS OF THE OLD WEST. THE GLASS DOORS COULD BE PULLED BACK TO OPEN THE CASINO TO THE SIDEWALK.

FREMONT AND FIRST STREETS, C. 1958. ABOVE-GROUND TESTING BEGAN IN 1951 AT YUCCA FLATS, SEVENTY-FIVE MILES NORTH OF FREMONT STREET, CHALLENGING THE NEON SIGNS FOR SUPREMACY OF THE SKIES. PUBLICITY WIZARDS MANAGED TO TURN THE PERILOUS BLASTS INTO A REASON TO VISIT LAS VEGAS.

Club), and typefaces suited to an 1850s wanted poster blown up and eerily radiating light. Only the nearby atom bomb blasts begun at the Yucca Flat testing range seventy miles away in 1951 challenged these signs for supremacy of the skies.

In the 1930s Fremont Street had been a mix of Main Street shops and a few casinos. By 1955 only one drugstore, one telegraph office (a vital adjunct to the casinos), and one bank remained on the street as the casinos expanded. The $6 million, thirteen-story Fremont Hotel of 1955 was built by established San Francisco hotelman Lou Lurie. Breaking the dominance of the Old West style, the state's tallest building was strictly modern. Designed by the prolific Wayne McAllister (who had a 1.5 percent share in it) with partner William Wagner, it brought Strip amenities and style to Fremont for the first time. It had a pool, a showroom, and hotel rooms. An excellent example of 1950s hotel design, it distinguished the large horizontal public spaces on the ground floor from the modular room units in a vertical slab. The tower was faced with a multicolored curtain wall system of interlocking concrete panels and sunscreens. Pinks and red-browns were integral colors. As a commercial architect, McAllister was at ease with signage (fabricated by YESCO)

and articulated the signs as separate blades hung on the top and side of the tower. While the Riviera was clearly Miami Modern, the Fremont Hotel was California Modern.

The Barbary Coast was not the only example of western Americana to be spun into a Las Vegas casino. In 1954 the Showboat opened on the Boulder Highway with one hundred rooms. A city report predicted the area would become a commercial center, and William Moore, the original architect and operator of the Last Frontier, built this casino to exploit it. Local architects Zick and Sharp worked with him. This showboat, in an ingenious evocation of its historical river habitat, plowed through a pool wrapped around its bow. A showboat may have appeared incongruous in the context of the desert, but it made sense in the context of gambling. The riverboat was a technological advance (the first steamboats appeared on western rivers in 1811 and continued to be used throughout the nineteenth century) which, as an unexpected side effect, created a new venue to spread

◆

FREMONT HOTEL, 1956, WAYNE MCALLISTER AND WILLIAM WAGNER. FREMONT STREET'S FIRST HIGHRISE, BY THE INFLUENTIAL WAYNE MCALLISTER AND HIS PARTNER WILLIAM WAGNER, WAS COVERED IN PINK AND REDDISH TAN CONCRETE PANELS.

gambling through the western frontier in the mid-nineteenth century. The juxtaposition of these "floating palaces. . . . furnished like a fancy New Orleans club," in historian John Findlay's description in *People of Chance*, with the rough and tumble of the frontier society and the wilderness landscape setting was also a precursor of mid-twentieth-century Las Vegas, where high-style casinos were brought to mass-market gambling. The Showboat was only the first of a fleet of paddle wheelers to dock at Port Las Vegas over the years.

Las Vegas' growth was not limited to Fremont and the Strip. "There is also a new galaxy of motels that are so splendid they are hard to distinguish from the first string hotel casinos," reported A. J. Liebling in *The New Yorker* in 1953. Lucius Beebe cataloged them in 1952 for *Holiday*: "The littoral of U.S. 91 for five miles south of town abounds in gaudy names and souped-up dazzlements: El Mirador, LaRue, Club Bingo, motels, drive-ins, neon signs, justices of the peace, frontier filling stations, first and last chance saloons, frontier hot dogs, frontier follies, bingo, blackjack, roulette, horse rooms, big six wheels, craps, floor shows, bungalows, haciendas and patios, cut rate parsons and wedding chapels." Ever since El Rancho opened, residential tracts had been growing in the subdivisions east of the Strip. They were spurred by the resorts; many middle- and upper-wage-scale employees and management lived near their work. Other sunbelt cities like Los Angeles, Phoenix, and Tucson were annexing suburban areas to in-crease their tax bases. The city of Las Vegas made its first attempt to annex the Strip in 1946, but was re-buffed by the organized efforts of hotel operators and residents who preferred the looser codes and lower taxes of the Strip. Later attempts at annexation also failed. The Strip was left to unfettered development.

The $15 million, three hundred room Tropicana, opened in 1957, continued the tradition es-tablished by the Flamingo in 1946. Located a mile past the Dunes and Flamingo, it seemed to be in the mid-dle of nowhere. Designed by Miami architect M. Tony Sherman, built by the Taylor Construction Company of Miami (who also built the Riviera), and

♥

fronted by Ben Jaffe of the Fontainebleau, it was designated "the Tiffany of Strip hotels." But the era of sophistication in the sagebrush was coming to an end. Compared with the aristocratic casinos and spas of Europe, those in Las Vegas had always been thoroughly democratic. The market depended on volume, not on high rollers alone, though the Flamingo, Desert Inn, and Tropicana had relied on Hollywood aristocracy to distin-guish them. The future, however, lay with the mass market, and the next hotel would under-score that direction. It was a market that didn't require tuxedoed waiters. It would also introduce a remarkable popular architecture. The Stardust, opening the following year, would turn the evolving neon sign into the architecture itself. With it the classic period of the Las Vegas Strip would reach its zenith

♣

Dunes, 1955. A classic American place as interpreted in Las Vegas: the pool ter-race of a re-sort hotel. The low motel wings offer private boxes overlooking the poolside pageant.

Tropicana, 1957, M. Tony Sherman. The Tropicana con-tinued the pattern of a strong road-side symbol—the large and small petals of the tulip-shaped fountain flashed in opposite directions with rose and aqua neon—and use of a porte cochere en-try to a sprawling casino, with two- and three-story room wings around the garden pool.

In all those streamlined facades, in all those flamboyant entrances and deliberately bizarre decorative effects, those cheerfully self-assertive masses of color and light and movement that clash roughly with the old and traditional, there are certain underlying characteristics which suggest that we are confronted not by a debased and cheapened art, but a kind of folk art in mid-twentieth-century garb.

J. B. JACKSON, "OTHER-DIRECTED HOUSES," 1956

Mass Market Stardust: 1958—1965

IN THE SUMMER of 1958, the year of a record seventy-seven aboveground atomic tests, the Young Electric Sign Company (YESCO) built a vision of heaven along the desert roadside. Stretching 216 feet long and 27 feet high, it displayed planets and comets from an undiscovered galaxy that pulsed neutrons and radiated cosmic rays. Mixing neon, incandescent bulbs, plexiglass, and painted sheet metal, the shimmering universe was brought to earth and the Strip.

The Stardust's sign was unique but not unheralded. The Flamingo's effervescent cylindrical sign towered over the Strip. The Sands sign was integral to the architecture. The roots of the Stardust sign also lay in the billboards of the roadside vernacular. The Mint sign constructed the year before on Fremont Street, neon's procrustean bed, culminated an exploration of scale, volume, image, and color in signs that increasingly blurred the line between two-dimensional signs and three-dimensional architecture. The Stardust sign went even further. It became the architecture.

The Mint pioneered new sign imagery by breaking away from the dated streamline pylons of the Las Vegas and Boulder clubs. Taking the entire facade as its domain, the Mint sign was three-dimensional, sculptural, and complex in animation. Compared with the Old West style encouraged by the Chamber of Commerce, the Mint, remembers architect Harris Sharp, "stunned a lot of people."

An existing midblock storefront between First and Second streets, one hundred feet wide, was remodeled for the Mint. A horizontal canopy sheltered the sidewalk, but the main feature was a swooping line that began on one edge of the building at the sidewalk, swept up through the canopy, arced down, and then shot skyward. It was eighteen feet wide at its widest and projected out from the face of the building. A shooting ribbon of white incandescent bulbs began at the bottom of the curve and followed the arc's trajectory until, eighty-two feet off the sidewalk, the sixteen-foot star burst into neon flame, dazzling with three-hundred-watt signal lamps at its tips—all in a matter of seconds. The entire facade was covered in rose neon that matched the synthetic automotive enamels used on the sheet metal.

Architects Walter Zick and Harris Sharp's charge from client Milton Prell, of the Sahara, reflected the competition that promoted the growth of Fremont's signage. "They said they wanted an unusual sign that could be seen all up and down Fremont," recalls Sharp. The architects gave YESCO a sketch of a tall pylon with a curving tail. Sign artists Hermon Boernge and Kermit Wayne fleshed out the design

♥

STARDUST, 1958.
THE STARDUST WAS
THE FIRST STRIP
HOTEL TO FORGO
THE PRESTIGIOUS
CIRCLE DRIVE, SPACIOUS LAWN, AND
BURBLING FOUNTAIN.
ITS ARCHITECTURE
WAS A BILLBOARD
THAT ADVERTISED
NOTHING LESS
THAN THE UNIVERSE
ITSELF.

♠

THE MINT CASINO, 1957,
ZICK AND SHARP.
A TYPICAL SKETCH USED BY
SIGN COMPANIES, YOUNG
ELECTRIC SIGN COMPANY IN
THIS CASE, TO SELL A SIGN
DESIGN TO A CLIENT. YESCO
COLLABORATED WITH THE
ARCHITECTS.

Where did the shape come from? "You just keep drawing until something clicks," says Sharp, "It's just an architectural ability architects gain when they go to school." As postwar graduates of the University of Southern California's School of Architecture (Louis Armét and Eldon Davis, primary proponents of the parallel Coffee Shop Modern style, were classmates), Walter Zick and Harris Sharp were familiar with the abstractions of modern architecture. But that hardly explains the radical leap to the Mint's electro-organic swoops. It far surpassed the rudimentary streamline touches on the early Boulder and Las Vegas signs. It had depth. It united the vertical pylon with the horizontal marquee. Two years later Zick and Sharp would expand the Mint to the site of the Birdcage casino at the corner of First Street (which had replaced the 1906 First State Bank in 1957). To do so they reinterpreted the original arc to make an arching eyebrow that masterfully turned the corner and created an urban landmark. This addition's Etruscan helmet shape echoed the 1957 Berlin Congress Hall of Hugh Stubbins, Jr., rendered in a popular medium.

The solution suited the downtown site. Packed cheek by jowl, the Fremont Street casinos had to grab attention by creating a sensation on their facade. The 1950 Golden Nugget sign used huge scale; the Pioneer used pictorial symbolism. But for the Stardust's Strip site, a different challenge confronted the sign designers. The neighboring casinos were not the competition. The night sky and the vast desert were. They could swallow a low sprawl of motel wings without a trace. Amid the dense crowd of Fremont Street buildings, the colors, shapes, and movement of neon could give identity to a building. Against the black Strip sky, a neon line could create a presence on the highway.

The Stardust began as another idea of Los Angeles gambler Tony Cornero. From his boat, the SS *Rex*, Cornero had "realized big profits weren't to be made from either the well to do or the big gamblers, but from the masses of middle class folks who could be coaxed aboard to play the slots or roulette. They demanded clean, attractive, well run premises, and this Tony provided. It was a lesson Las Vegas learned from Tony Cornero," writes historian Bruce Henstell in *Sunshine and Wealth*.

The mass market was in Cornero's sights when he organized the Stardust company in 1954. Its strategy was to step away from the country club elegance of the Desert Inn and Sands to broaden Las Vegas' appeal. His customer, said Cornero, was "looking only for fun, entertainment. And that's what I give him." Cornero schemed that by charging $5 a day for rooms and giving guests $5 for gambling, he could turn a profit. He sold hundreds of shares in the company—with irregularities that attracted the attention of the Department of Justice.

Not modern, not western, the $10 million Stardust was architecturally little more than a warehouse. "Tony Cornero's Starlight" it was originally to be called, and it was to have its own train stop on the Union Pacific track bordering its rear property line. The train station never materialized, but the vastness of the project did. It was billed as the largest hotel in the world, and whether or not it was, it was still breathtaking: one thousand rooms in two-story wings that stretched to the rear of the thirty-two-acre property like boxcars at the freight yard;

a 105-foot pool; and a 16,500-square-foot casino. Though it has not been positively documented that he conceived the huge billboard facade, it fitted Cornero's iconoclastic approach.

But Cornero would never see the Starlight—renamed the Stardust. In a Runyonesque finale, he died in the saddle, of a heart attack while gambling at the Desert Inn in July 1955. The unfinished shell sat empty almost two years while the asking price came down. Then Moe Dalitz, Allard Roen, and their Desert Inn associates took over the Stardust operation for financial backer Jack Factor, brother of Max Factor. The architecture of the partially completed hotel was as chaotic as Cornero's financing. No one was in clear command, remembers Thomas Turner, engineer with the newly hired architects, Jack Miller Associates of Las Vegas.

It is likely that the Stardust was initially designed largely by the engineer or the contractor. The design was a collection of individual functions (motel wings, casino, showroom) without an overall concept or image. It did not attempt a unifying roof like the Desert Inn's, or an elegant entry like the Flamingo's. Nor did it have a focal porte cochere like those of the lowrise Dunes and Tropicana. The structure of the main building was tilt-up concrete walls, covered with wood roofs, a favored method for warehouse and industrial buildings, buildings typically designed without architects. The two-story motel wings were post-tensioned concrete slab structures, another efficient industrial building technique. T. Y. Lin, who would distinguish himself for advanced engineering work, engineered the structure of the motel wings.

Turner reports that it was a difficult job. Decisions were postponed; information filtered down slowly. It was hard to get the many people involved together to decide anything. Functional problems became quickly apparent. It was discovered that the already built casino ceiling did not allow for an attic story for surveillance of the gaming tables. Jack Miller Associates took the existing shell and designed the kitchen, restaurant, upstairs ballrooms,

♦

THE MINT, 1957, ZICK AND SHARP. THE MINT'S SPECTACULAR THREE-DIMENSIONAL SWEEP INTRODUCED ARCHITECTONIC VOLUME TO THE GRAPHICS OF FREMONT STREET SIGNS. UNDER THE SIGN, PETRIFIED WOOD VENEERED THE WALLS.

and Aku Aku restaurant (a separate tiki-style, A-frame flanked by Easter Island heads), and revamped the showroom for the lavish Lido de Paris show. That enormous theater boasted a stage containing three hydraulic lifts, a truck dock, a rain curtain, a waterfall, a thrust stage wrapping around seating in pits, and a tilt-up half-inch mirrored plate-glass floor that reflected aquacade swimmers in a pool below stage. It was a stage that could easily feature the sinking of the Titanic, and in one memorable stage production, it literally did.

For interiors Moe Dalitz brought Jac Lessman, the interior designer who had worked on the Desert Inn in 1950. "It's the biggest anything I have ever seen, and I include the Jama Mosque of Delhi. . . . Its cavernous lobby is a wild jamboree of games of chance and those

♣

LEFT: **STARDUST, 1958.**
THIS SPRAWLING COM-
PLEX ENCOMPASSED THE
OLD ROYAL NEVADA
HOTEL (LEFT), THE TIKI-
STYLE AKU AKU RESTAU-
RANT (CENTER), ONE
THOUSAND MOTEL ROOMS
LINED UP LIKE BOXCARS
(TOP), AND THE STRIP'S
LARGEST SIGN, 216 FEET
LONG.

taking a chance on them," wrote Horace Sutton in *Saturday Review*. By the late 1950s a common formula had been hammered out for the design of casinos and hotels, says architect Jack Miller who worked on the Stardust. The casino was the first thing you saw when you entered; all other functions, from hotel check-in to restaurants to showrooms to pools, spun off this center.

The Stardust soon took over the neighboring Royal Nevada, which had gone bust. Slightly remodeled, its showroom became an auditorium for the Stardust, and its rooms were added to the burgeoning mega-motel. A half circle was added to the Royal Nevada's roofline, but the fountain of neon tubing marking the entry was saved.

The Stardust was already partly built when YESCO was hired to design and fabricate the sign. The construction supervisor, a retired admiral, asked YESCO and other sign companies to propose a selection of signs for the facade plus the roadside sign. On occasion, YESCO would hold a design competition among its artists, as it did for the Stardust. Kermit Wayne's design was selected for both the facade and the roadside signs.

With so many fragmented elements spread across a huge lot, the sign was crucial to the design. It became the Stardust's architecture by default, yet was no accident. Freed from architectural convention, from sophistication, even from exotic and Old West themes, the Stardust offered nothing less than a panorama of the solar system that exploded beyond the edges of the building. At the sign's center sat a plastic earth (sixteen feet in diameter, formed in slices three feet across), ringed by a

Sputnik off the front pages of the newspaper. Cosmic rays of neon and electric light bulbs pulsed out from behind the earth in all directions. Three-dimensional plexiglass planets spun in the ether alongside twenty scintillating neon starbursts. Plastered across this universe was a jagged galaxy of electric lettering spelling out "Stardust." The *S* alone contained 975 lamps. By day the sky's painted sheet metal looked deep sky blue; on a clear night the neon constellation was reportedly visible sixty miles away.

At roadside stood a second freestanding sign: a circle constraining an amorphous cloud of cosmic dust circled by an orbit ring and covered in dancing stars. The hotel's name was nestled in a galactic cloud; the attraction board advertised the Lido de Paris ("60 stars, Exciting Acts, Gorgeous Girls"). Coordinated subsidiary signs marked out the domain of the Stardust at secondary entrances. The roadside sign was no larger than the Desert Inn's and Flamingo's, which were also circular.

The Stardust's facade was bent in the middle slightly to conform with the building. The southern half angled back to face northbound traffic. The sign was hoisted aloft one story on a colonnade of stone pillars similar to the Desert Inn's. Display windows with bezels

RIGHT: **FREMONT AND
SECOND STREETS,
c. 1957.**
"THE HIGH AND CONTIN-
UOUS FACADES [OF
FREMONT STREET] MAY
BE ONLY AN ILLUSION
MADE WITH LIGHT, BUT
THEY ARE MORE CON-
VINCING THAN MANY AN
ATTEMPT TO CREATE THE
SAME KIND OF EFFECT,
THE SAME PEDESTRIAN
DOMINANCE, BY MEANS
OF SOLID AND CONVEN-
TIONAL ARCHITECTURE,"
WROTE REYNER BANHAM
IN 1970.

lined the arcade, and other larger billboards, announcing restaurants and other attractions, hung on either side of the sign.

The rest of the building, an unassuming two- and three-story structure, peeked out hesitantly from behind this brazen sign. Lacking the Desert Inn's lawn and fountain, or the Riviera's dramatic front drive, the front of the Stardust was a parking lot with a sign, like any Ralph's market.

Ten years later, *Learning from Las Vegas* authors Robert Venturi, Denise Scott Brown, and Steven Izenour would identify this striking building type as a decorated shed, a relatively simple structure with an elaborate but independent layer of symbolism to organize urban space. Historical examples abound, from the cathedral at Orvieto to the Palazzo Farnese. The decorated shed proved a critical element for strips. The

♥

GOLDEN NUGGET, 1957. KERMIT WAYNE CARVED A TWELVE-INCH MODEL OF THE NUGGET'S BULLNOSE CORNER FROM BALSA WOOD.

Stardust took this urban form further than it had ever been taken before.

A Kermit Wayne anecdote may shed light on the origin of the idea of turning an architectural facade into a billboard. One day after the Stardust's completion, Wayne was at the Desert Inn talking with a friend, a pit boss. They decided to drive over to the Stardust, when a man walked up and asked for a ride. As they drove up in front of the glittering Stardust sign, the man pointed to it and said, "You know, I designed that sign." Wayne, possessing the pride of accomplishment, told the man in clear terms that he, Wayne, was the artist. The man said no more, but after he left, Wayne's friend turned to him and said, "Do you know who that was?" "No," said Wayne. "That was Moe Dalitz," replied the pit boss. As the Stardust's primary partner after Cornero's death, Dalitz may have promoted the sign to focus the unorganized jumble Cornero left behind.

Though Dalitz may have claimed authorship, the facade sign was reportedly part of Tony Cornero's original concept. It suited the bigger-is-better design philosophy seen in the hotel's one thousand rooms and enormous casino. Whoever originated the idea, it was dictated by the building's commercial role and strip site. But it took on a larger meaning as other hotel designers realized its effective roadside strategy.

The sign's gigantic size made sense by strip requirements, which demanded visibility in a strip's grand sprawl. The choice of a concrete tilt-up structure, which lacked the formal possibilities of the earlier ranch-style motels, dictated the need for ornament to create identity. The nonarchitectural imagery was borrowed from the front pages, not from the region or history. It recognized architecture as a mass medium, not just a structural medium. This idea had been developing in Las Vegas. It is rooted in the old western false-front building. The Stardust put them all together, intensified by Kermit Wayne's brilliant exploitation of the artistic possibilities.

What prompted the innovative design? Wayne is indirect. "I was thinking of my wife in the hospital with a chronic problem," he says. That along with the constant tension at work produced the energy apparent in the design. The Sputnik was his idea, he says, as was the sequencing of the lights to mark the satellite orbit on the roadside sign, thereby creating the illusion of a trail of light behind the orbiting satellite. The result was accomplished with color and deftness, with boldness and delight that burst through the confines of convention, as commercial vernacular design can, to make something that could appeal to child or adult. It was a magnificent excuse to turn light, neon, and exploding animation into a pure, nearly abstract image. So vividly did the Stardust sign symbolize the populist taste of Las Vegas that it acted as a lightning rod for critics: "Its tinseled facade resembles a Dali nightmare," wrote Ed Reid and Ovid Demaris in *The Green Felt Jungle*. This is the commercial vernacular design process.

The Stardust would be the last Strip hotel to be built in the 1950s, but it set off a cycle of remodeling and additions. Its influence reverberated down the Strip in the next ten years. In the wake of the opening of the 1959 Convention Center, hotels sought conventioneers as a mix of business and pleasure marked the emerging postindustrial city.

This was the era of the big signs, soaring more than 180 feet into the sky in front of the Dunes, the Stardust, the Sahara, the Frontier. It was the era when free-form design from the fingertips of the sign makers turned the Horseshoe into an icon of 1950s design and the Golden Nugget into a Victorian fantasia. Unhampered by a sense of shame, unrestricted by fashionable architectural theory, they produced the Las Vegas of "Boomerang Modern, Palette Curvilinear, Flash Gordon Ming-Alert Spiral, McDonald's Hamburger Parabola, Mint Casino Elliptical and Miami Beach Kidney," as Tom Wolfe codified the phenomenon for *Esquire* in 1964. Also during this era, the gaps in the Strip began to fill in as parking lots disappeared and hotels and casinos edged out toward the sidewalk.

These major remodelings would change the face of the Strip. But before they did, a tie to its earliest days was severed: El Rancho Vegas burned mysteriously in June 1960. The first Strip hotel, it was the pioneer that opened the Strip to plush resorts and established the motel as the basis for Strip development. In the late 1950s it had not been able to keep up with the trend to modernize; steep mansard roofs had been added to its gently sloping shingled roofs to increase its visible presence on the Strip. El Rancho's outlying bungalows, untouched by the fire,

remained for a few more years until they were sold and moved.

Just as Fremont Street's Mint had been father to the Strip's Stardust sign, the Stardust concept bounced back to Fremont Street in the early 1960s. Signs started to swallow buildings. The first to be gulped was the Golden Nugget, remodeled in 1957 by one of the Renaissance men of neon, YESCO's Kermit Wayne. The Golden Nugget began a new era of Glitter Gulch signage so powerful that it would imprint the neon image of Second and Fremont streets in the global imagination. Some citizens, worried about Las Vegas' gaudy image, rechristened Glitter Gulch as Casino Center in an attempt at upgrading. Fortunately good taste did not stem the town's freewheeling populism.

The Golden Nugget went from cowboy Victorian to neon Victorian. After an in-house competition at YESCO, Wayne's design was selected. The large frame sign overhead remained, but it was given a pedestal with a huge bullnose of opulent Lillian Russell proportions rendered in neon. The two street facades along Second and Fremont were covered for one hundred feet in neon tubing; every few seconds each facade would be swept in rose and blue hues. The floriated borders of Victorian ornament were rendered in jumping neon.

" 'We want that 1890 flourish,' clients would say. Then it's almost automatic that you come up with something like that," Kermit Wayne recalls about the Golden Nugget design. "I rarely went to books [for design or lettering ideas]." The designs existed in the artists' and the mass audience's memories and were instantly recognizable. "There was a lot of stuff in town with that Barbary Coast style," he remembers. The Old West lettering with block serifs, the ornate curlicues and twists, and the fragmentary fleur-de-lis all echoed the past rendered in high tech. "Casino" was framed by running incandescent bulbs over the corner. Above it sat a scintillating nugget the size of a small car. The date 1905 was in neon, rather than carved stone. The design made a monument of the heavily trafficked corner, gave the Golden Nugget a startling image that remained in the memory, and defined the sign as architecture itself. Joining the Flamingo's champagne tower, the Stardust sign, and the Mint sign, it became an indelible image of American popular culture.

Continuing the Gold Rush theme next door was the 1954 Lucky Strike Club, which followed in the location of the Frontier Club.

Twin miners panned for gold above a Barbary Coast marquee. In 1961 this was remodeled by YESCO into another shimmering icon of Modernism: the Lucky Casino, whose highrise neon facade shot up into a thin tower topping out at 157 feet, the name sprawled in classy script over the orange neon tubing. By the late 1960s it would be swallowed by the expanding Golden Nugget and its electric Victorian facade. The Nevada Club (later Diamond Jim's) and the Western Union office on the block also disappeared behind the neon curtain. In the 1980s the Golden Nugget's framed "Casino" on the Second Street corner was replaced with a sixteen-color animated sign advertising the delights within. "The high and continuous facades may be only an illusion made with light, but they are more convincing than many an attempt to create the same kind of effect, the same pedestrian dominance, by means of solid and conventional architecture," noted Reyner Banham in the *Los Angeles Times* in 1970.

The early 1960s brought a rash of facade remodeling to Main Streets everywhere. Victorian and Art Deco facades disappeared under expanded-web screens of gold anodized aluminum, or were stripped of terra-cotta ornament. In Las Vegas the Pioneer Club elected the former route, placing a basket-weave anodized aluminum screen over its stucco facade. Twenty years later, fashions once again swung away from Modernism back to historicism, and the screen was removed. The Horseshoe remodel was more elaborate. It followed the Golden Nugget in turning the old Hotel Apache at Second and Fremont streets into a neon sign and expanding into the neighboring Boulder Club, which had burned in 1956. The architects were Wayne McAllister and William Wagner, though McAllister had just left the partnership to take a position

with the Marriott Corporation. The architects sorted through several of YESCO's proposals to create the final design. The brick three-story hotel disappeared under a field of flashing neon and incandescent bulbs fabricated by YESCO. Light splashed along doglegs and evaporated into the neon atmosphere on spikes—lightning rods in reverse. Located across the street from the Golden Nugget's convex bullnose, the Horseshoe added a concave billboard of interlocking H's. In sharp contrast to this modernity, Old West typeface replaced the 1940s Detroit auto-modern script typeface along the marquee.

Once the Horseshoe swallowed the old Boulder Club around 1960, it and the neighboring Mint made a solid block of superb 1950s popular Modernism. Neon had outgrown two-dimensional graphics and was entering a shimmering new life in three dimensions. This ultramodern technology created glass houses not to see through, but to be seen. World's fairs, especially Chicago's in 1933, experimented with the architectural possibilities of neon. Yet nothing had been as bold as this block of Glitter Gulch.

♠ ♦ ♣ ♥

BY THE 1960S, casino owners realized that specific architectural equations translated into profitable hotels. A certain number of rooms meant a certain number of customers losing money at the casino. Those rooms had to be within easy walking distance of the casino, so highrises became part of every hotel game plan. Highrises proved more efficient and reliable than astronomical salaries for headliners as a way to attract large numbers of gamblers. Elevators were placed so that customers had to walk through the casino to get to them. Restaurants, lobby, and entertainment were all accessible from the casino, which became the central plaza of the hotel. Casino cages were located away from entries to make robberies more difficult. Each hotel tried to keep the customers in their own casinos, and the distances from hotel to hotel helped. So did air-conditioning.

♠

LUCKY CASINO, 1961. TOWERING OVER FREMONT STREET, THE LUCKY CASINO FACADE FEATURED TWO CURVING SECTIONS MEETING AT AN EDGE CONTINUOUSLY TRAVERSED BY TRAVELING LIGHTS. THIS IS ANOTHER YESCO PRESENTATION MODEL.

Proximity to newly opened Interstate 15, which paralleled the Strip a half mile to the west, also figured into the game plan.

The highrise invasion of lowrise Las Vegas began in the late 1950s. The anomalous Riviera strayed from the Miami beachfront in 1955 and the fifteen-story Fremont Hotel rose on Fremont Street in 1956. During this first decade of towers, they were so few and far between that they had the status of landmarks—the sense of a skyscraper, as Louis Sullivan had defined it, as a slender and isolated shaft in a horizontal landscape. Many were as shapely, if not quite as sculptural, as the highrise signs that accompanied them.

The first highrise after the Riviera was the Sahara's fourteen-story tower, designed by Los Angeles architect Martin Stern, Jr. This 1959 expansion included a convention hall on the Sahara's north side and a 127-foot vertical roadside sign by YESCO. The tower, set on the far side of the pool, was patterned with windows, balconies, and stair towers that imparted a dynamic, sculptural quality. A digital time and temperature board and the semi-Arabic S were perched on top. Stern designed a twenty-four-story tower for the Sahara in 1963.

The ten-story Desert Inn tower, built in 1963 by New York architect William Tabler, accompanied a major remodeling of public spaces, restaurant, and showrooms. Tabler, architect of the postwar Statler Hotels in Washington, D.C., and Los Angeles, and formerly with the Chicago architectural firm Holabird and Root, also designed the nine-story Stardust tower, operated by the same management. They bear a familial resemblance. The Desert Inn tower stood directly north of the casino, replacing the original room wings designed by Wayne McAllister. The cloud and cactus sign that had topped the Sky Room was hoisted to the top of the new tower. Its one hundred rooms and suites were expressed in an eggcrate pattern of balconies and windows on east and west facades. In the middle of the Desert Inn's expansion period, founder Wilbur Clark died, in August 1965.

None of these initial towers were as innovative as the highrise that had been under construction since 1961, off the Strip on Paradise across from the 1959 Convention Center. The Landmark Hotel was another project plagued by lack of financing. It grew out of the parking lot of a corner shopping center and served as apart-

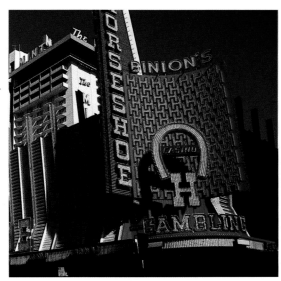

♦

HORSESHOE CLUB, 1962, WAYNE McALLISTER AND WILLIAM WAGNER. THE ARCHITECTS ASKED FOR CONCEPTS FROM THE SIGN ARTISTS, AND THEN COMBINED THEM IN THE FINAL DESIGN.

ments before opening in 1969 as a casino. Originally planned as Nevada's tallest building at fifteen stories, the hotel was by 1964, as a result of the efforts of the hopeful builder, Frank Carroll of Kansas City, a thirty-one-story tower that projected Las Vegas into the high-tech future outlined at the 1962 Seattle World's Fair by the Space Needle. The architect was Edward Hendricks of Los Angeles, later with the firm of Daniel Mann Johnson Mendenhall. This stylized mushroom had pie-shaped rooms in its stem (as in Bertrand Goldberg's 1962 Marina towers in Chicago) and was capped by a lens-shaped capsule with outriggers tapering to fine points. The capsule held the bar, restaurant, and casino. The dome echoed that of the 1959 Convention Center across the street. It was meant to stand alone and heralded a potential future of desert skyscrapers as weird and shapely as the new generation of signs.

That future never arrived, but it did leave one unbuilt project worthy of note: Bruce Goff's Viva Hotel of 1961. Plumbing the depths of the national consciousness, Goff's sublimely organic and lavishly ornamental designs belong to the same end of the spectrum of American design that includes such forbidden aesthetic fruit as Las Vegas' gaudy populist neon architecture.

The twenty-two-story Viva tower had a triangular plan. Each

successive story was cantilevered out slightly from the floor below, giving the building's form an organic energy. Spiral stair towers hung from each point like confetti streamers. Clad in white stone aggregate, the concrete structure was trimmed in white neon. A feathery porte cochere welcomed people below. At the tower's base three oval pods contained entry, casino, showroom, and restaurant. The center of the tower was open, an early proposal for an atrium lobby with elevators rising through its center. A topknot, shifted sixty degrees off the tower's triangle, held terraced suites and the Rocket Room sky bar graced by wagon wheel–shaped windows. Oval bungalows and circular cabanas were scattered around the hotel's base.

The Viva Hotel was to have been built on the northern half of the Strip at Fulcher. The client, Viva Ruth Liles, lost a prime financial backer in a plane crash and the Viva joined the long list of unbuilt projects in Las Vegas. Intriguingly, the three-winged plan was repeated at the International Hotel in 1969 and the Mirage in 1989.

Like much of Goff's work, the Viva would have astonished and outraged. A tentative admirer, *New York Times* critic Ada Louise Huxtable, called it Space-Camp. But it remains a summation of the possible direction Las Vegas might have taken had more architects and clients exploited the extravagant lack of restraint strip design permitted. The Viva's silhouette would have rivaled the best of the Strip's shimmering signs as an unashamedly artificial feature in the desert wasteland. Its original ornament had the freshness and daring associated with the

other great artists working on the Strip, the sign artists of YESCO, Ad-Art, Federal Sign, and others. The mirrored glass of today's Desert Inn and Mirage seeks only to reflect some of the Strip's surrounding glitter; the Viva would have radiated its own beatific glitter.

The Viva was never to be, but mainstream Modernism's great set piece would be built for the Dunes in 1964. It was also something of an anomaly on the Strip, but added a notable flavor to the blend of western, commercial, and contractor vernaculars that made up the mix of the Strip.

The lowrise 1955 Dunes motel was turned into a resort complex dominated by another new highrise, the twenty-one-story Diamond of the Dunes by Chicago architect Milton Schwartz. More than doubling the hotel's number of rooms (which rose from an initial 200 to 450 in 1961), the addition was styled like many other large hotels circa 1960, spurred by the growth of jet travel. Las Vegas, too, could now be reached by a wider pool of visitors; McCarran Airport had opened a new terminal domed for the space age in 1962.

Unlike most other Strip hotels, the Dunes expansion was part of a long-range master plan allowing for five future towers and intending to turn the Dunes into a major resort. As the architect of a series of highrise apartments and hotels, University of Illinois graduate Schwartz designed the kind of well-crafted mainstream modern buildings in which Chicago has specialized. Deftly contrasting cleanly cut aluminum cladding with balcony insets, the Chicago Loop's 1956 Executive House

♣

PAGE 76 LEFT: **THE STRIP, 1962.**
THIS IS THE CLASSIC STRIP: A RIBBON OF HIGHWAY THAT LINKS THE ARCHITECTURE. THE BUILDINGS THEMSELVES FADE INTO THE BACKGROUND, AND THE WIDELY SPACED SIGN PYLONS BECOME THE LANDMARKS DISTINGUISHING ONE PLACE FROM ANOTHER.

PAGE 76 CENTER: **SAHARA, 1959, MARTIN STERN, JR.**
THE FOURTEEN-STORY TOWER WAS BALANCED BY THE NEW VERTICAL SIGN AT THE MAIN ENTRY. BY THIS DATE THE MODEST SCALE OF LAS VEGAS' ORIGINAL SIGNS, LIKE THE SAHARA'S 1952 BRICK PYLON SIGN, WAS BEING ECLIPSED.

PAGE 76 RIGHT: **LANDMARK HOTEL, 1964, EDWARD HENDRICKS.**
THE TROUBLED LANDMARK PROJECT DID NOT BECOME A CASINO UNTIL HOWARD HUGHES BOUGHT IT AND OPENED IT IN 1969. IT BELONGS TO A BRIEF PERIOD WHEN THE NEW HIGHRISES ALMOST ACHIEVED THE FORMAL EXUBERANCE OF THE SIGNS.

THIS PAGE: **VIVA HOTEL, 1961, BRUCE GOFF.**
THE VIVA, AN UNBUILT PROJECT, INTEGRATED THE HIGHRISE TREND OF THE EARLY 1960S WITH THE AESTHETIC OF THE GREAT SIGNS OF THE SAME PERIOD.

♥

DUNES HOTEL, 1964, MILTON SCHWARTZ. THE DIAMOND OF THE DUNES IS A CLASSIC PIECE OF EXPRESSIONISTIC MODERNISM, DOWN TO THE ABSTRACT PATTERNS IN THE ROOFTOP GRAVEL AND THE PORTE COCHERE SPIRES. IT STANDS IN A LANDSCAPE OF COFFEE SHOPS, BILLBOARDS, MOTELS, AND THE NEWLY OPENED I-15 FREEWAY. NOTE CAESARS PALACE UNDER CONSTRUCTION BEHIND THE DUNES SIGN.

Hotel had a facade that seemed neatly machined. Dunes owner Jacob Gottleib, Chicago shipping magnate, liked the Executive House and hired Schwartz to remodel the existing Dunes (adding convention rooms and the Sultan's Table restaurant) and then to develop a master plan. A golf course was also added.

Though it was a concrete frame structure, the Diamond of the Dunes was creased on its two broad sides like the side panel of a 1963 Buick Riviera, and, like the Executive House, appeared machined. Deeply inset balconies protected the windows from the heat of the sun while giving an indoor-outdoor character to the highrise rooms. A nightclub and health club occupied the penthouse. Without possessing the Landmark's techno-romance or the Desert Inn tower's prosaic up-to-dateness, the Dunes managed to project the elegance and progressiveness of Modernism. The diamond shape had been used, in variation, by Le Corbusier for a vast highrise project for Algiers in 1938, by Walter Gropius and Marcel Breuer for Manhattan's Pan Am building in 1958, and by Gino Ponti and Pier Luigi Nervi for the Pirelli Building in Milan in 1960. Schwartz denies having been aware of those as models for the Dunes, though in retrospect he sees similarities in the designs from the same era.

Gottleib remained close to the project, approving everything and flying to Las Vegas frequently with Schwartz. Also closely involved was the lessee of the Dunes' casino and entertainment operation, Major Riddle. In trying to upgrade the class of people the hotel attracted, de-

sign was considered critical, and Schwartz was attentive to details down to the colors, tablecloths, and blue martinis of the Sultan's Table.

Fleshing out the picture, Schwartz added a new porte cochere and a new seafood restaurant, the Dome of the Sea. The Dome was one of the fantastic possibilities of which Modernism was capable: a clamshell of a room suspended from six legs of sculptured concrete by a web of stainless steel threads. The legs sat in a free-form pool of water that reflected onto the bowl-shaped underside of the structure. Inside, set designer Sean Kenney, who had worked briefly with Frank Lloyd Wright, continued the undersea theme by projecting fish, seaweed, and subaqueous images on the walls. A small stage held a harpist in a Siren suit. Schwartz specified all details: a five-foot, six-inch blonde, dressed in white and gold, was to sit in a large seashell that moved through a pool on a figure-eight track.

The Dome of the Sea belongs to a strain of late 1950s Modernism that explored the sculptural potential of concrete. From Oscar Niemeyer's 1941 Church of St. Francis of Assisi in Pampulha, Brazil, to Eero Saarinen's 1962 TWA terminal at Idlewild Airport in New York, to John Lautner's 1959 Silvertop house in Los Angeles' Silver Lake, to Pereira and Luckman's 1962 Theme Building at Los

♠

FREMONT STREET, 1965. HIGHRISES GREW ON FREMONT STREET IN THE 1960s. THE MINT'S TWENTY-SIX-STORY TOWER WAS BUILT IN 1965, AND THE FREMONT HOTEL ADDED AN EXTENSION IN 1963. THE FOUR QUEENS IS UNDER CONSTRUCTION IN THE FOREGROUND. THE NEON TOWERS OF THE LUCKY, MINT, HORSESHOE, AND LAS VEGAS CLUBS PROVIDED A MEDIATING SCALE WHEN VIEWED FROM THE SIDEWALK.

Angeles International Airport, these buildings were frequently derided as willful expressionism, as mere googie. Many East Coast critics, with their taste for the austere, could not fathom such exuberance. But it was this wing of Modernism that permitted exploration and play, not the austere International Style, to which Las Vegas looked.

Completing the picture at the Dunes was a signature porte cochere. Twin tapering pylons swept skyward in an evocation of dynamic lightness. It was, in fact, designed on Schwartz's many five-hour flights from Chicago to Las Vegas on TWA's twin-boom planes. "I wanted something outstanding, needless to say, something that would soar, lift the spirit. . . . It was my feeling of what it would be like to enter this fabulous world," he explains.

Inside the Diamond of the Dunes, the festive fantasies of the restaurants and bars were enhanced by an elegant use of sleek technological materials—stainless steel for elevator doors and stainless-coated carbon steel rods suspending floating stair treads—balanced by rougher, more colorful materials such as the glazed inch-square ceramic tiles used in accent walls. Butterfly-wing folded panels hung from the ceiling as baffles. Had the Diamond of the Dunes been built on Chicago's Lakeshore Drive, it might have been considered mainstream Modernism. Built on the Las Vegas Strip, it lost its individual identity and became part of the general Strip landscape of excess.

The Dunes was, in fact, a more lively essay than most contemporary examples of corporate Modernism. The 1957 Nile Hilton in Egypt and the 1958 Havana Hilton in Cuba, both by Los Angeles' Welton Becket Associates, who designed a nine-story wing in 1959 for the Riviera, were dominated by rectilinear highrise slabs far less fluid than the Dunes. Only lobbies, restaurants, and terraces were alive with domed ceilings, suspended curving staircases, asymmetrical public spaces, and walkways canopied with zigzag folded-plate roofs. The Dunes, like Morris Lapidus' 1959 Summit Hotel in New York, carried a similar energy to the city skyline.

The Dunes and Summit were surpassed by one of the new highrise hotels in a competing gambling center, Havana, Cuba. The twenty-one-story 1957 Havana Riviera, bankrolled by Ben Siegel associate Meyer Lansky, was an even more skilled and adventurous modern

◆

DUNES HOTEL, 1964, MILTON SCHWARTZ. THE DOME OF THE SEA, ORIGINALLY SITTING IN A DECORATIVE POOL OF WATER, WAS AN EXPRESSIONISTIC JEWEL BOX FOR A SEAFOOD RESTAURANT.

design, allowing curving concrete floor slabs to project out past the surface plane of the glass. The tower was clad in turquoise mosaic. An oval-shaped gold-tiled dome patterned with swirling abstract designs hovered over the casino. A planar roof and angled freestanding walls created a daring free-form porte cochere. With 440 rooms, it was the largest casino hotel outside Las Vegas. Irving Feldman, a Miami builder, constructed it in less than a year. Al Parvin, who also worked for and had interests in Las Vegas hotels, did the interiors. Two years later, with Fidel Castro's victory, all casinos were closed in Cuba.

The same highrise trend affected Fremont Street, where the Fremont Hotel added a fourteen-story tower (by Zick and Sharp, with Wayne McAllister as consulting architect) in 1963. The Mint opened a twenty-six-story tower with three hundred rooms, designed by architect Martin Stern, Jr.; as at many of Stern's hotels, the upper floors were wider than the lower ones to allow for spacious suites. The Sundance opened a nine-story tower with 176 rooms in 1965.

Even more significant to Las Vegas' evolution as an urban form were the giant signs that grew alongside the highrise towers. The great neon landmarks of Las Vegas—the Golden Nugget facade, the freestanding Stardust sign, the Dunes signs—are all products of this era when the logic and grammar of Strip design were maturing.

Hermon Boernge, Ray and Jack Larsen, Jack Larsen, Sr., Lee Klay, D. W. Norman, Kermit Wayne, and Ben Mitchem are a few of

♣

STARDUST, 1965. AS IT EXPANDED, THE STARDUST REMODELED ITS ORIGINAL FACADE AND ADDED ONE OF THE GRANDEST OF THE GREAT ROADSIDE SIGNS OF THE MID-1960S, A STRIP CAMPANILE FOR A ROADSIDE SAN MARCO.

the names belonging on the long list of unsung sign artists. A catalog of their major designs covers a significant portion of the spectrum of American design. Their work is as large as the western landscape and as pragmatic as an assembly line. Their art draws deeply from our common memory, but also transforms it with their idiosyncratic visions. Their medium is technology and commerce.

The careers of these sign artists were hardly glamorous. Few people considered their work art at all. As Tom Wolfe found in 1964, the artists drew on no conscious tradition. Often they were treated with indifference or contempt by their company's salesmen. Most of their work involved ordinary commercial signs that they churned out on a regular basis. Yet despite such constraints, these artists were able to create indelible images in a cohesive aesthetic that integrated architecture, advertising, and culture. Perhaps they even thrived because of the limits of the marketplace. They occasionally worked with budgets large enough to allow them to stretch their medium. Neon never went out of fashion in Las Vegas, as it did elsewhere.

The backgrounds of the sign artists vary. In the early days only a few had professional academic training. Most were commercial artists and sign painters. Jack Larsen worked for a time at Disney Studios. Kermit Wayne's biography is typical: Born in 1914, Wayne painted theatrical posters and placards ("It's 20 degrees cooler inside") for the Balaban theaters in Chicago during the Depression. After serving in Italy

in World War II, he went to work for MGM Studios in Culver City as a scenic artist, painting with twenty other artists the huge illusionary canvas murals of landscapes, cities, or skies that served as backdrops on a soundstage. It was an education in scale, a necessity for an urban sign designer. Wayne worked on *Quo Vadis* and *On the Town*, where his top-of-the-Empire-State-Building view of Manhattan focused prophetically on the neon signs of New York. When movie-making moved off the studio lots to real locations in the 1940s and 1950s, Wayne relocated to Las Vegas. There he painted lobby placards for shows at the hotels. At the Last Frontier in 1957, YESCO's Jack Young offered him a job. Ready to try something new, he accepted. Though he had never touched a tube of neon before, he made the extraordinary shift from intimate, two-dimensional graphics to urban-scale three-dimensional neon with confidence. In a range of signs, from the abstract Mint, to the space-age Stardust, to the baroque Golden Nugget, to the classical Caesars Palace, Wayne's work displays a spectacular imagination and a variety of line that combines instantly evocative popular images with formal dexterity. He retired from YESCO in 1976.

Sign companies are a sales business, not a design business, and friction between the artists and the salesmen could be intense. Rarely

♥

DUNES SIGN, 1964. THE GREAT SIGNS THAT SHAPE OUR IMAGE OF LAS VEGAS AS A CITY OF NEON TOWERS WERE ALL BUILT IN A RELATIVELY SHORT PERIOD IN THE MID-1960S. LEE KLAY OF THE FEDERAL SIGN AND SIGNAL COMPANY DESIGNED THE DUNES SIGN.

would artists be given credit. Salesmen met with clients to discuss what kind of signs were needed, sometimes sketching designs themselves in the clients' offices. Or a salesman would relay the client's desires to the artists back at the office. Rarely did the artists have direct contact with the clients.

Relations between architect and sign artist varied. In some cases the architect would design a sign and the sign company would simply fabricate it. Many architects, however, had an aversion to signs, preferring to think that their buildings make a sufficient statement without the addition of cluttering words and logos. The building owner would often commission and approve a sign design without consulting the architect. In important jobs like the original Stardust sign, YESCO would hold a competition among its own staff to generate a range of creative ideas. Because of the great cost of signs, they were leased to the hotels rather than purchased.

The artist would create for the client a rendering of the design, in colored paint on black paper to simulate night. Sometimes a model would be built, too. Once the design was approved (often after several proposals), the designer would tell the engineers what animation they wanted in the sign. In the 1950s and 1960s, all the flashers were mechanical with cams and wheels that turned each individual bulb or grouping on or off. The engineers would also determine how to frame and secure the sign, and how to fabricate the fanciful curves the designers often stipulated. To fabricate the fiberglass shoe for the Silver Slipper, they bought a high-heel shoe, filled it with plaster, and then cut it into sections that could then be measured and scaled up, a technique one of the engineers had used in designing airplane fuselages.

Many of the basic animation effects have changed little since the beginning of the century. Bulbs or tubes are turned on or off, in random sequence to achieve a scintillating effect, or in a strict sequence to give the appearance of a traveling light. The technology, however, has changed greatly, from hand-switching in the early decades of the century to computerized animation today. What has also changed is the sophistication of the effects as sign artists explored the possibilities. Initially signs simply blinked on and off to attract the eye. Later, traveling lights were used to draw the eye to the casino's entry for obvious

♠

FRONTIER SIGN, 1967. THE LAST VESTIGES OF THE 1942 LAST FRONTIER HOTEL WERE REPLACED IN 1967 BY THE FRONTIER HOTEL, WHICH ALSO BUILT ONE OF THE GREAT SIGNS OF THE 1960s.

commercial reasons. But in the 1964 Dunes' geyser of boiling neon, or the original 1958 Stardust's cosmic rays, or the intricate waves of rose and blue hues sweeping across the facade of the 1957 Golden Nugget, the imagination of the artist is at play.

Often more than one sign company would bid on a job, and each would come up with a design. YESCO, headquartered in Salt Lake City and one of the largest companies in the region, met real competition for the first time when the California sign maker Ad-Art moved into town in 1965. Before, Local Neon and Western Neon were the competition.

Signs underwent as many updates and expansions as the hotels and casinos themselves. Secondary signs sprouted at secondary entries to parking lots; attraction boards doubled and tripled in size and number. Signs grew in size as competition for the biggest raged. The Sahara led the way with a slender 127-foot sign in 1962. Signs also grew in expressiveness. Stand beneath the great sign of the Dunes some hot evening and watch the neon flame erupt silently into the sky. It sparkles and then in a microsecond evaporates, only to begin its trajectory into the sky once again. The silence of these giants is eerie. They have the elemental quality of streaks of lightning that rivet our attention on the summer horizon—but without the affirming crack and rumble a few seconds later. Contributing to this dreamlike state is their apparent disregard for physical law. The light leaps off the ground faster than a rocket, turns corners with incredible precision, and reverses direction with unnatural ease. It is all illusion, of course, accomplished with the sequential

◆

THUNDERBIRD HOTEL, 1965.

THE LONGEST SIGN IN LAS VEGAS, THIS FREE-STANDING BILLBOARD HAD LETTERS THAT STOOD OUT ON A BED OF GOLD LIGHT, ECHOING THE SHELL SIGN ACROSS THE STREET. BEHIND IT THE OUTLINES OF THE ORIGINAL HOTEL CAN STILL BE SEEN. COMPARE THIS WITH THE PHOTOGRAPH OF THE THUNDERBIRD IN CHAPTER THREE. THE ANGLED SIGN ABOVE THE PORTE COCHERE WAS THE HOTEL'S THIRD GENERATION OF ROADSIDE SIGNS.

flashing of tubes and bulbs to give the appearance of movement. It is no less effective for being illusory.

When the Stardust added a nine-story tower in 1964, it remodeled its landmark facade, expanding as had other casinos out into the parking lot by the highway. The new facade, by Ad-Art, continued the galactic theme, but raised the Stardust name, still in electra-jag letters, onto a pole above the exploding universe. The rest of the facade was treated as an abstract neon tapestry.

In 1965, a new roadside sign, replacing the old circular roadside sign, became a classic image of American popular architecture. The Stardust's original signs had been informed by the plasticity of the roadside sign tradition, where signs took the forms of boats, cows, or frying pans as the occasion demanded. The new 1965 Stardust sign, designed by Ad-Art at a cost of $500,000, suggested something beyond itself. Its form was blurred by a scatter of star shapes around its periphery. It depicted, in fact, a shower of stardust. At night, in the animation sequence, light fell from the stars, sprinkling from the top of the 188-foot-tall sign down over the Stardust name, igniting a subatomic frenzy within them and then showering down onto the for-

tunate people below. It was a stupendous and joyful image. Incorporating neon and incandescent bulbs, it was designed by Paul Miller, who had previously worked for Raymond Loewy.

Equaling the Stardust in roadside grandeur is the 180-foot Dunes sign of 1964 designed by Lee Klay of the Federal Sign and Signal Company, at a cost of $250,000. Its simple form and riveting animation create a major and unforgettable American icon. The onion dome silhouette evokes a *Thousand and One Nights* fantasy, but when it is read as a stylized spade, the sign reflects the roadside tradition of buildings in the shapes of the things they sell, like a hot dog stand in the shape of a giant hot dog. With electric lava erupting through the sign into the sky every minute, the Dunes sign is phenomenal.

The architect of the Dunes, however, didn't want it. Milton Schwartz objected to the sign's size, shape, and placement in relation to his Diamond of the Dunes. He had designed a spire sign that tied in with the porte cochere. Major Riddle, who ran the hotel, demanded a sign to keep up with the new generation of signs on the Strip. Schwartz fought it. Riddle fortunately won. In Strip style, it is a conglomeration of commercial needs and people's taste that creates successful architecture.

Hotel expansions continued unabated through the 1960s. In the 1950s the Thunderbird revamped its uptown ranch house with a modern, flat-roofed expansion. After Del Webb bought it for $10 million in 1964, a new facade was created south of the original entry: the seven-hundred-foot sign stretching across the old room wings south of the entry was the Strip's biggest, over three times as long as the 1958 Stardust's. Nonpictorial, it simply framed the name on a background of golden light.

In 1965 the last remnant of the seminal Strip, the original Last Frontier, was razed for a completely new hotel. Called simply the Frontier, it opened in 1967 with its own great sign. In 1962, at the height of the swingers' Las Vegas, the Sands added the U-shaped three-story, eighty-three-room Aquaduct wing (all room wings were named after racetracks) at the rear of the property. In 1965 the Sands added a seventeen-story cylinder tower topped by a tiara of looped arches ringing the penthouse. It stood prominently along the still mostly lowrise Strip. At its base, the original 1952 Wayne McAllister casino was re-

SANDS TOWER, C. 1967,
MARTIN STERN, JR.
WAYNE MCALLISTER'S TWO-
STORY MOTEL WINGS REMAINED,
BUT STERN'S SEVENTEEN-STORY
CIRCULAR TOWER ECHOED THE
CHANGE IN SCALE AND HEIGHT
ALONG THE STRIP IN THE
MID-1960S.

TALLY HO, 1962.
THE TUDOR ROOM WINGS OF
THE OLD TALLY HO SERVED THE
THOUSAND AND ONE NIGHTS
FANTASY OF THE ALADDIN. ONE
EXPECTS SUCH IMAGE COLLISIONS
ON THE STRIP.

modeled into a plainer, less elegant facade that included a smaller cylinder sheathed in colorful mosaics, and a new triangular porte cochere. Martin Stern, Jr., was the architect.

Not all hotels were going highrise. The 1962 Tally Ho motel aimed to prove that a resort motel without a casino could be successful. Tudor style, it had leaded windows, gables, and half-timbering. It failed within a year. An attempt in 1964 to make it work as the King's Crown failed after six months. Low motel wings still were popular for expansions; the Flamingo and Thunderbird added restrained versions of the versatile Los Angeles stucco box, with flat roofs, elegantly set windows, and traces of decorative structure. On the Boulder Highway far off the Strip, the Showboat expanded every few years through the 1960s, adding motel wings and alleys to its bowling emporium, which cemented its reputation as a favorite of local residents.

In 1966 Milton Prell, one of the original owners of the Sahara, reopened the failed Tally Ho as the $16 million Aladdin, adding a casino and the Bagdad Theater along the highway in a flat-roofed structure. Prell swapped the Tally Ho's Olde English imagery for an Arabian Nights theme, but kept the original Tudor room wings with 335 rooms. A serrated canopy cantilevered over the front entry was,

other than signage, the only embellishment. Contributing to the design's surreality was a $750,000 fifteen-story sign, a loopy Aladdin's lamp that pushed the boundaries of sign design. Ray Larsen, Jr., designed it for YESCO. The new sign maintained the high standards of the signs at the Dune and the Stardust.

Las Vegas achieved a vivid and conceptually strong urban framework in the early 1960s. The overgrown motels of the early 1950s evolved into large complexes accommodating theaters, terraces, highrises, convention centers, and multiple expansions. In the great signs, the Strip had developed an urban aesthetic that proved both practical and expressive. They were conceptual gateways, guiding drivers down the Strip while telegraphing the experience to be discovered inside. As landmarks, signs gave order to the parking lots, lowrise casinos, motel blocks, and few highrise towers strung along the highway. They proved as effective as the church spires and city hall domes of traditional cities. In Times Square, neon signs had been decorative wallpaper on existing buildings. In Las Vegas, the signs shaped space itself. "Las Vegas and Versailles are the only two architecturally uniform cities in Western History," wrote Tom Wolfe in 1965.

Las Vegas was the only city of its kind to be seen on this scale or thoroughness. To call it untraditional would be an understatement; it was generally considered an urban freak, in thrall to the gigantic and the garish. But Las Vegas was not done inventing itself. In the next phase, hotels would be embellished with images and styles that made them islands unto themselves.

♥

ALADDIN HOTEL, 1966.
MILTON PRELL, WHO OPENED
THE SAHARA, RETURNED TO LAS
VEGAS TO ADD A CASINO TO
THE FRONT OF THE FAILED
TALLY HO, OPENING IT AS THE
ALADDIN. YESCO'S SIGN WAS
A FREE-FORM PHANTASM INCOR-
PORATING HINTS OF JEWELRY,
VEILS, MAGIC LAMPS, AND
FANTASY.

All characters once dead, if they continue to exist in memory at all, tend to become fictions. Hamlet is no less real now than Winston Churchill.

GRAHAM GREENE, **TRAVELS WITH MY AUNT**, 1969

5

Beyond the Wildest Dreams of any Roman Emperor: 1966—1980

IT WAS ROME and it was not Rome. As with a dream, only a few cues were required to convey the place's identity. Caesars Palace needed only a sumptuous array of Classical statuary and a host of marble-white columns to establish its theme. The visitor's imagination, in league with well-placed publicity, filled in the opulence.

The $25 million Caesars Palace, opened in August 1966, summarized the state of the art of Strip design in the mid-1960s. Rarely resorting to overt authenticity, entrepreneur Jay Sarno and Miami architect Melvin Grossman conjured up a broad yet highly detailed Classical environment suited to the large and lavish expectations of Las Vegas gamblers. The first new hotel to be constructed in eight years broke from the roadside motel tradition to introduce a plan borrowed from Baroque cities. The usual frontage parking lot was amended by a long axis of fountains marking an entry drive; the parking lots were pushed to the side for this grand effect. The focus was on a monumental structure with symmetrical wings reaching out to embrace the limousines cruising up to the porte cochere. Above loomed a convex fourteen-story tower. There were 680 rooms.

The motel prototype used for most Las Vegas resorts since 1941 called for buildings to be arranged casually on the site. A sign or facade was likely shifted to face oncoming traffic. Caesars faced the Strip with a royal presence and bulk that established its own organization in its own domain. It disdained accuracy in favor of vigor. Technically speaking, the wings that marked the entry were more Baroque Rome (they took the parabolic shape of St. Peter's Square) than Imperial Rome. The statues and fountains evoked the Villa d'Este and other summer villas of Baroque cardinals in Tivoli. Such lapses have to be excused; a resort more accurately named Popes Palace would not have drawn as many gamblers.

Jay Sarno had planned to build the Cabana Palace in Las Vegas, the flagship of his nationwide Cabana motel chain. Soon rechristened Caesars Palace (the studied lack of apostrophe emphasized that anyone in the mass market could be a Caesar with this as his palace), Sarno's dream enveloped visitors in a total environment intended to transport them from reality to fantasy. He practiced this in his other motels. The 1961 Palo Alto Cabana in California, a small-scale version of Caesars Palace, features a long axial entry off the commercial strip of El Camino Real, a curving facade faced in black granite, and wings faced in two stories of glass. Behind sits a nine-story tower faced in a patterned screen.

Under Sarno's guidance, Melvin Grossman repeated all these elements. Grossman, no stranger to revisionist historicism in design, walked a tightrope between new and old in his luxurious Acapulco Princess Hotel, a modernized Mayan pyramid that appeared to be in the initial stages of ruin because of its covering of jungle vines. At roadside, at the head of the spraying fountains at Caesars, stands a copy of the Winged Victory of Samothrace. The main

♠

CAESARS PALACE, 1966, MELVIN GROSSMAN.

IF IT WAS ROMAN, IT WAS THE SUMPTUOUS SPLENDOR AND GRAND PROSPECTS OF BAROQUE ROME, NOT CLASSICAL ROME, THAT JAY SARNO AND MELVIN GROSSMAN IMITATED.

◆

filigree surface faces the fourteen-story tower behind. Buried deep within this fantasy, though, was a typical roadside motel. Low room wings circled the pool terrace on the west side of the hotel. And at roadside stood a sign.

Mirroring a national trend to soften Modernism, Grossman used motifs pioneered by architects Minoru Yamasaki and Edward Durrell Stone. In the 1964 Northwestern National Life Insurance building in Minneapolis, Minnesota, Yamasaki updated the Parthenon's symmetries and colonnades. Classical columns were abstracted as fluid, tapering stems melting into arches. Stone's conscious effort to to return applied ornament to modern architecture resulted in the kind of grills and screens seen at Caesars for the 1954 U.S. Embassy in New Delhi. Yet Caesars Palace cannot be dismissed as derivative any more than the Golden Nugget's electric Victorian style can be dismissed as imitation Victorian. Caesars was a true popular culture appropriation of high-art forms overtly mixed with historical forms in a way a high-art architect never would have done in this period. "Roadside copies of Ed Stone are more interesting than the real Ed Stone," observed architects Robert Venturi and Denise Scott Brown. Caesars proved it.

Sarno asked for proposals from local sign companies for the new sign. Young Electric submitted an entry, designed by Jack Larsen and Kermit Wayne, which ripped a pediment, architrave, and columns off a Roman temple and placed them at right angles to the road. Originally two attraction boards laced through the four Ionic columns; later a single, bigger board and two freestanding columns for support were added, "a feat never attempted, a problem never solved in the whole evolution of Classical architecture," marveled the authors of *Learning from Las Vegas*. The result is emblematic of the attitude of theme architecture. The artists used enough of the vocabulary of Classicism to make the images recognizable, then stretched that vocabulary to serve a new cultural context. The columns are too large for a temple, but just right for a Las Vegas sign.

building is set back an impressive 135 feet. The original porte cochere was a flat canopy backed by a black-tiled screen, flanked by reproductions of Classical statues in scalloped niches. The low wings on either side are screened with a filigree of open concrete blocks behind a modernistic colonnade of tapered columns rising from planters. The same

For the design's presentation, Larsen and Wayne visited a dime store and picked out a few toy soldiers for scale; they happened to be centurions. Sarno liked them so much that he insisted that full-scale, full-color figures of vestal maids and plumed centurions be added to the base of the actual sign. As pedestrian traffic has increased in recent decades on the Strip, the fiberglass soldiers and maids have become a sidewalk attraction.

At the last moment YESCO chief Thomas Young turned down the job because of the shaky finances of the clients, who balked at paying half the cost before beginning fabrication. Ad-Art then stepped in and did the job with no money down for $350,000. The design was essentially the same as YESCO's.

Just inside Caesars' entry, a vast, low casino dominated the interior. Its shallow oval-shaped dome hovered over the gaming pit. Windowless and with a blacked-out ceiling, the casino relied on sparkling trim lights to give it shape, though not substance. Its unusual shape and visually magnetic materials echoed the interiors of master Modernist Oscar Niemeyer's public buildings in Brasilia. Around this central oval spun a welter of shops, restaurants, lounges, and corridors. Some paths led to the Noshorium Coffee Shop or to Cleopatra's Barge, sitting in its own miniature Mediterranean. Others led to the sunlight,

made more blinding by the dazzling white exterior. One corridor went to the twelve-hundred-seat Circus Maximus, the main showroom. The plan tempted visitors to wander in search of new delights, a quality that has increased as the casino has expanded. In this conglomeration of outdoor and indoor spaces, Caesars came closest to a Roman model, Emperor Hadrian's Villa in Tivoli. Choosing a rich complex of spaces and styles, that Caesar devoted rooms and gardens to different parts of the world to remind him of his empire. Even the builders of Monte Carlo's casino knew the value of making pleasant places to promenade within sight and sound of the casino's attractions.

By the time of Caesars' construction, the Strip was no longer a random collection of unrelated buildings. The roadside had evolved a loose organization that defined an emerging urban form. "The Strip . . . is grandly a string of island palaces in a sea of dark, connected by a canal of leisurely automotive transport," wrote Reyner Banham in 1970 in the *Los Angeles Times*. Each hotel/palace, separate but equal, faced the common highway across a parking lot. Interspersed with these large complexes were smaller motels, gas stations, rental car lots, and souvenir shops. Except for a handful of highrises, the buildings hugged the ground. Public space was divided between car-oriented areas outside and pedestrian-oriented areas inside. The great signs had been born as creatures of this landscape to establish an identity and focus the Strip.

♣

CASINO, CAESARS PALACE, 1966, MELVIN GROSSMAN.
THE LOW, BLACKED-OUT CEILING, MIRRORS, AND GLITTERING TRIM LIGHTS OF CAESARS' OVAL-SHAPED MAIN CASINO BLURRED THE BOUNDARIES OF THE CASINO AND CENTERED ATTENTION ON THE PEOPLE, NOISE, AND ACTION. THE RESULT WAS AN AURAL AND VISUAL WORLD OF TENSION AND MOVEMENT—A VIVIDLY DEFINED PUBLIC SPACE.

Just as the highway was becoming Roadtown, the first serious study of Las Vegas as an urban form was undertaken by Yale University professors Denise Scott Brown, Robert Venturi, and Steven Izenour. Scott Brown had discovered Las Vegas first, while teaching at the School of Architecture and Urban Planning at UCLA. Like Reyner Banham, who was also a foreigner, she could see the city in ways most native Americans could not. In March of 1968 Scott Brown and Venturi published their initial thoughts on the city in *Architectural Forum*, and in the fall

brought a group of architecture students to analyze and document the phenomenon. Their timing was excellent; they arrived in town just as the Strip had evolved and perfected an urban form of signs, symbols, and vast space. Pop Art had already exposed commercial and vernacular objects to the scrutiny of high-art culture. Architecture finally caught up. In 1972 the treatise on their findings, *Learning from Las Vegas*, was published.

But Las Vegas was already changing. Caesars Palace gave the strip medium a message by perfecting a critical element of the Las Vegas style: theme architecture. Theming had been present since the days of El Rancho Vegas' windmill. Fremont Street's Golden Nugget and Pioneer Club had continued the tradition, but the Strip hotels of the 1950s drifted away from it. Despite the Congo Rooms, the Casbahs, and the plaster camels, the Sahara, Dunes, and Sands were not theme designs so much as posh, modern commercial designs. Caesars represented the culmination of the trend to unify the vacationers' visit by designing every detail of what they saw and experienced. The hotels existed as much in memory and fancy as in time and place, and were intended to intensify the experience of a place. The Strip was becoming a string of such worlds.

Caesars showed that the landscape of southern Nevada was of less and less interest to Las Vegas' promoters. In the 1940s and 1950s the natural wonders and recreational delights of nearby Lake Mead and Mt. Charleston had been prominent in Chamber of Commerce brochures. But the lesson of air-conditioning had been learned. Even the most terrible conditions of the environment could be redesigned. The desert was a blank slate, an empty soundstage on which any story might be presented. With Caesars, Las Vegas themes shifted the spotlight to exotic times and spaces. This shift had a practical purpose. Psychologically, the fantastic resorts distanced customers from the everyday world and the concerns that might put a brake on their gambling, notes gambling historian John Findlay.

Of course, underneath the theme, the island palaces were cut from the same cloth. All were, in fact, large decorated warehouses with clanging slot machines, felt-topped tables, restaurants, and theaters. Each resort offered basically the same pleasures, and each casino offered exactly the same odds on identical games. The margins were slight, which meant each hotel had to attract a mass audience. Theming offered one way for a hotel to differentiate itself from the pack.

Theming began to preoccupy the thoughts of Howard Hughes soon after he moved to Las Vegas in November 1966. The man for whom the term "reclusive billionaire" was invented sought to become the most powerful man in Nevada. Ensconced in the Desert Inn's penthouse floor, cut off from light and all but his immediate guard, he was immensely powerful for a while, but he turned out to be a transitional character in the development of Las Vegas.

With over $500 million from the sale of TWA Airlines, Hughes began buying hotels. He may not have had a clear idea of what he was going to do with the money when he arrived secretively in Las Vegas one night. He may only have been looking for a place to hide from the subpoenas generated by his legal battles. But he had an idea of what Las Vegas was about. Before he left he owned the Desert Inn, the Frontier, the Silver Slipper, and the Landmark.

"I like to think of Las Vegas in terms of a well dressed man in a dinner jacket, and a beautifully jeweled and furred female getting out of an expensive car. I think that is what the public expects here—to rub shoulders with V.I.P's and stars, etc.—possibly dressed in sports clothes, but if so, at least good sports clothes. I dont [sic] think we should permit this place to degrade into a freak or amusement-park category, like Coney Island," he wrote in a memo to his lieutenant, Robert Maheu, as quoted in Michael Drosnin's book *Citizen Hughes*.

It was an echo of Ben Siegel's twenty-year-old vision. Hughes had frequented the Flamingo in the early days, and for his 1952 production of *The Las Vegas Story* with Jane Russell, Victor Mature, and Vincent Price had used the "Flamingo to represent all that is glamorous and exciting about Las Vegas . . . as the example of the grandeur and the luxury of plush gambling on the Las Vegas Strip." The exterior of the Richard Stadelman room wing doubled as the front of the fictional hotel, the Fabulous.

Howard Hughes was wildly more successful as a buccaneer than Ben Siegel ever hoped to be, but both shared a personal vision of Las Vegas. Yet Hughes would be no more successful in seeing his vision prevail. To Hughes' horror, one of the Strip casinos opening in 1968 actually had a Coney Island–style merry-go-round as its sign on the Strip. Jay Sarno built the $15 million Circus Circus casino as another pointed bid to attract families to Las Vegas. Architects Rissman and Rissman Associates designed a giant, pink-and-white, oval-shaped circus tent across from the Riviera. The roof followed the curves of draped canvas, and pennants ringed its crown. Acrobats performed trapeze and high-wire acts over the heads of gamblers playing in the gaming pits below. To separate the gamblers from the children as required by law, a second level contained midway games and attractions in view of the circus acts. It was open to all with the price of admission.

"The aspect of The Circus that has me disturbed is the popcorn, peanuts and kids side of it. . . . And also the Carnival Freaks, and Animal side of it," moaned Hughes. "In other words, the poor dirty, shoddy side of Circus life. The dirt floor, sawdust and elephants. The part of a Circus that is associated with the poor boys in town, the hobo clowns, and, I repeat, the animals. The part of a circus that is synonymous with the common poor man—with the freckled face kids, the roustabouts driving the stakes with three men and three sledge hammers, etc., etc."

The exaggeration of Caesars Palace and the populist extrava-

ganza of Circus Circus drew a battle line between competing visions of Las Vegas in the late 1960s. After years of borderline existence, living from bust to boom and back, through scandals and murders, many citizens thought the town had finally become respectable.

From Ben Siegel to Wilbur Clark to Howard Hughes to today's Steve Wynn of the Mirage, Las Vegas has attracted entrepreneurs who believed in the marketability of sophistication. It has also had Tony Cornero, Jay Sarno, and the Excalibur's William Bennett, who believed in appealing to the mass market and mass taste. Both visions have contributed to the shape of the town. The difference today is that sophistication has become one more theme to attract a market share. With three thousand rooms, the Mirage must attract a mass audience to survive.

Hughes was fighting an uphill battle. With his immense investment he hoped to control growth and keep Las Vegas exclusive; it was better business, he thought, if room reservations were difficult to get. Yet his mere presence made the city appealing to other investors. To many people he symbolized a new era that had thrown off the mob

♠

FLAMINGO, 1967, MARTIN STERN, JR. PUSHING OUT TO THE HIGHWAY FRONTAGE, THE FLAMINGO'S LATEST REMODELING GAVE IT A COVERED PORTE COCHERE, A SKY-ROOM RESTAURANT ABOVE IT, AND A NEW, PINK-PLUMED ROADSIDE SIGN. THE CHAMPAGNE TOWER WAS HISTORY.

influence of the past and cleaned up Las Vegas with his organization of Mormons and former FBI men. In fact, that was mostly cosmetic, as Moe Dalitz still ran the Desert Inn's casino even after Hughes bought it. Scandals still lay in the future. High rollers alone were not enough to keep the city afloat. Unwittingly Hughes was inviting in the mass market he loathed.

So Hughes became a transitional figure. He belonged to the earlier era of individual entrepreneurs like Hull and Siegel and Clark and Cornero who could influence the shape and style of a hotel on personal whim. Yet with his bankroll he also carried the clout of a corporation. He made Las Vegas respectable and stable for corporate investment. To become Strip City, Roadtown had to change. It needed new and larger financial sources. It needed people with managerial experience to weather the leap in scale. Hughes supplied both. Though Del Webb had enjoyed a corporate presence in Las Vegas for many years, Hughes' name and example made it possible for Hilton, Holiday Inn, Ramada, and other large groups to invest and operate in Las Vegas. The days of experiment were ending. The Las Vegas package was becoming more standardized as a commodity. That was to be the future.

When he skipped town in 1970, Hughes had not built a single hotel. Las Vegas was in a building boom during his years there, but Hughes had been a buyer, not a creator. Just after Hughes moved into town, the Riviera opened an eleven-story wing designed in 1965 by Los Angeles architect Harold Levitt. In 1967 the Frontier, soon to be a Hughes acquisition, reopened with a completely new building by Rissman and Rissman Associates with 650 rooms and a $500,000, 186-foot roadside sign by Bill Clarke of Ad-Art.

Another tycoon who was to have an even greater long-term impact on the Strip bought his first hotel in 1967: airline owner Kirk Kerkorian purchased the Flamingo for $13 million, demolished the legendary 1953 champagne tower, added a three-hundred-seat theater,

expanded the casino, and housed it behind a new two-story porte cochere. A glass-enclosed restaurant on the upper floor overlooked the Strip. Martin Stern, Jr., was the architect. The Flamingo edged toward the sidewalk on its increasingly cramped site. Faced in a checkerboard of marble and mirror, this latest remodeling lacked the sleekness of Pereira and Luckman's 1953 facade. The rococo of the 1950s was being replaced by rectilinear lines. A boxed fascia shading floor-to-ceiling glass echoed the simplified lines of many commercial and office designs of the period. A set of new plumed signs standing at roadside retained the same reverse-*F* name plate. They were designed by Ad-Art's first art director, Bill Clarke. Kerkorian used the Flamingo as a staff training ground for his next project, the International.

A tri-winged tower that was the largest in Las Vegas and possibly the free world when it opened, the International, designed by Los Angeles architect Martin Stern, Jr., bore a superficial resemblance to Bruce Goff's unbuilt Viva Hotel of 1961. Even though the International had broad curving facades, its sleek, contained style lacked the Viva's excitement. The articulation of stair towers, of corner windows, of penthouses as sculptural elements in a composition, seen in the early Riviera or in Stern's own Sahara towers, was missing. The curving porte cochere was sculptural in the manner of corporate office buildings

of the 1960s. Though big, it was understated, in contrast to Las Vegas convention. A second-floor terrace topped the low casino and meeting rooms. In size and simplicity, the International showed the way to the future. It had fifteen hundred rooms, a thirty-thousand-square-foot casino, and cost $60 million.

Each floor had a different nationality theme, but the International was not truly theme architecture. Other hotels were facing the problem of adding on to already cramped sites, which resulted in a hodgepodge of additions. The International, sited on the old racetrack property east of the Strip, had the luxury of spaciousness. The original scheme called for three smaller, tri-winged towers to be built at the tip of each of the three main wings, a rational expansion plan allowing the new to blend almost seamlessly with the old. As built, however, the expansions were simply carried in a straight line from the original wings.

The International, along with the neighboring Landmark Hotel which finally opened as a casino two days before it in July 1969, promised to establish a second strip along Paradise Road. A comparison of the early architecture on the Strip and that on this newer strip reveals the impact of the motel prototype on the Strip's form. Without the discipline of a highway site, these new hotels became large, sculptural objects, isolated on their sites and symmetrical on all sides. Neither had a front to face the street and oncoming traffic. As singular, self-contained forms, they showed none of the complexity of the different pieces and sequential additions that made the original Strip visually and urbanistically richer.

During Hughes' Las Vegas stay, the successful Caesars Palace added the fourteen-story Centurion tower on its north side in 1970. Soon after Hughes left town, the corporate consolidation began. In 1972 Caesars World bought the Thunderbird, and Holiday Inn opened a thousand-room hotel fronted by a paddle wheeler next door to the Sands; the architect was Rissman and Rissman Associates. Encouraged by Hughes' presence in the gaming capital, Hilton Hotels moved in,

♥

MGM GRAND, 1973, MARTIN STERN, JR. GLITTERY PLASTIC COFFERS EDGED THE PORTE COCHERE. OVERSIZED RAILINGS LED UP BANKS OF STEPS. THE VAST CANOPY COULD COVER A FLEET OF LIMOUSINES. THIS WAS THE PORTE COCHERE OF THE FUTURE.

buying first Kerkorian's International in 1970 and then the Flamingo. The stake helped bankroll Kerkorian's next project, the lavish twenty-six-story MGM Grand Hotel which opened in 1973. The architect was Martin Stern, Jr.

Stern had stepped into the shoes of the departing Wayne McAllister as one of the most influential and prolific architects in Las Vegas. McAllister, designer of the milestone El Rancho, Sands, and Fremont, left his partnership with William Wagner to take a position with Marriott Corporation in the East. Stern began his Las Vegas career in the mid-1950s, designing a two-story motel wing on the south side of the Sahara. But before coming to Las Vegas, both architects had established active and influential commercial practices in the homeland of strip architecture, Los Angeles. Like many other Los Angeles architects, Stern had been a sketch artist at a movie studio in the 1930s. He worked for Paul Williams, and also for William Gage on the 1932 Spanish Colonial Beverly Hills City Hall. By the early 1950s he was a successful architect based in Beverly Hills who had designed housing tracts, apartments, coffee shops, and bowling alleys. His Ship's coffee shops in Culver City (1957) and Westwood (1958) were classics of Los Angeles car-culture design. The link is significant. Stern, Wayne McAllister, and Douglas Honnold all contributed to a highly tuned popular roadside style of signs,

♠

**FLAMINGO HILTON,
C. 1977, RISSMAN AND
RISSMAN ASSOCIATES.**
THOUGH THE NEW TOW-
ERS, BEGUN IN 1972, HAD
THE NEUTRAL APPEARANCE
OF OFFICE BUILDINGS, THE
SIDEWALK WAS ENLIVENED
BY ONE OF THE BEST NEW
SIGNS IN YEARS.

bold shapes, and modern imagery in the 1940s and 1950s in Los Angeles. These strategies proved fruitful to these architects when they began designing the larger, more complex Strip casinos.

The MGM Grand was the face of the new Strip. Big and brassy in the Las Vegas tradition, it introduced efficient forms, appealing materials, and ornament and themes that the corporations in Las Vegas could embrace. It walked the same fine line between grandeur and populism as the old movie palaces that provided its theme.

An L-shaped tower sat 350 feet back on the property next to the 1967 Bonanza hotel. In front lay the broad roofs of the casino, shopping arcade, and lobby, punctuated by the Aztecan truncated pyramid of the main showroom. The room tower was topped by an irregular pattern of windows and balconies, finished in mirror glass, indicating the variety of suites and rooms inside. The spacious casino was finished in the oversized gilt floral swirls and baroque ornament of a 1920s movie palace. Yet the space, despite these cues, did not have the same sense of triumphal procession that the original movie houses enjoyed.

The new tone of Hughesian sophistication was summed up in the MGM's single greatest architectural contribution to the Strip style: the porte cochere. The porte cochere had been in Las Vegas since the Thunderbird debuted in 1948, though it had not been de rigueur. The

Desert Inn did not have one originally, and the Flamingo did not build one until 1967. The most elegant, as might be expected, was at the 1952 Sands, with slender fins jutting out of the roof and diving into the ground.

In the 1970s, portes cocheres became important in Roadtown as symbols of elegant arrival by car. The porte cochere was the front door of a Strip building. Arrival was a ceremony officiated by a costumed doorman. A porte cochere magnified the front door to a size visible from the highway. Even many simple motels had portes cocheres for guests to park beneath out of the sun as they registered. Before the MGM, portes cocheres were either wide and western, held aloft by stone pillars, or slender and modern, like the Riviera's upswept canopy. The second Sands entry had a free-form canopy supported by single thin pylon. The Dunes had Brazilian Modern pylons sweeping up and out over the drive. The Stardust had a simple flat plane lifted on two columns.

The MGM redefined the Las Vegas porte cochere and with it Las Vegas style. Though Stern often left such details to his staff (Berton Severson designed much of the MGM Grand), he became personally involved in the design of the one-hundred-by-three-hundred-foot porte cochere. Its eight lanes could easily shelter a fleet of limousines. Ornate railings and balustrades were scaled to make it feel even larger. For the first time, the porte cochere replaced the roadside sign in projecting the primary imagery of a Strip hotel. The success of the MGM porte cochere blunted the race for bigger and flashier signs.

Incandescent point lights borrowed from movieland marquees, in keeping with the MGM's theme, were set in mirror-finish plastic coffers rimming the edge of the porte cochere. These light boxes multiplied the shimmery brilliance of each bulb. The shiny gold-and-silver-finish vacuum-formed plastic tended to warp and distort reflections, contributing a sense of ephemerality. But the point lights also had the effect of dematerializing the mass of the large structure, which seemed to lift almost effortlessly. Designers like Stern were eager to find new applications and visual effects for new materials like vacuum-formed plastic,

♦

CIRCUS CIRCUS, 1975, RISSMAN AND RISSMAN ASSOCIATES, PORTE COCHERE BY LEE LINTON. A DEFTLY SCALED AND AMAZING NEW MARQUEE SEEMED TO FLOAT OUT OVER THE ENTRY.

recently made available to the sign industry. Las Vegas was broadening the definition of glitter as it helped to invent glitz, a style to be explored in discos nationwide during the 1970s.

The MGM Grand's 125-foot sign, designed by Stern and Ad-Art, was also a trend-setter in the evolution of Las Vegas signage. Ad-Art designer Charles Barnard's first proposal showed a 207-foot dagger-shaped superpylon that would have been the Strip's tallest. It featured an 80-foot chandelier and called on all the tricks in the sign designers' book: scintillating lights, animation, neon, revolving lights, and incandescent raceways. While it continued the tradition of the great Stardust, Dunes, and Frontier signs, it would have gone even farther by contributing to the pedestrian environment at sidewalk level. The sign sat on a 16-foot-high concrete base with steps up its side permitting access to an 8-foot-high gold-finish fiberglass lion.

Though MGM General Manager Fred Benninger liked it, he vetoed the sign because of the extravagant price: $700,000. Ad-Art and Stern then proposed the current squarish design, which Stern favored because it competed less with the porte cochere and building. The decision would have a long-lasting (though unplanned) impact on the Strip. After the MGM, the focus of Strip design shifted from the sign to the portes cocheres. Where the Dunes sign across the street moved and

shimmered, the MGM's had no animation. Where the Stardust sign was shapely, the MGM's was squarish. The sign's slightly sloping edges echoed the pyramidal shape of the theater.

Most of the expansions and highrises of the 1970s borrowed the MGM Grand's modified corporate Modernism. Cleanly cut, abstract blocks made them modern; the tasteful facades that corporations wished to present to the public were styled with a monumental simplicity. The design committees of the corporations buying into the Strip were increasingly making architectural decisions. They felt comfortable with a style that was aesthetically safe and reliably inexpensive. The concrete and steel construction technologies were the same as those used in corporate office towers, and the hotel additions looked ever more like office buildings. They used simple lines and squared-off fascia overhangs, and, though large, were indeterminant in their scale. Only a few themed touches like mansard roofs, turrets, or signage dripping down twenty floors distinguished these corporate highrises as Las Vegas hotels. The energetic form giving of the Diamond of the Dunes or the circular Sands tower was absent. The new generation of towers dramatically changed the urban space of the Strip by hemming it in with walls. This compression of space also permitted the greater concentrations of people needed to make casinos profitable and a city possible.

As the MGM opened, other hotels were already expanding. In 1973 Caesars Palace opened a fifteen-story tower and the Hilton added fifteen hundred new rooms. The Flamingo Hilton added its first tower, by architects Rissman and Rissman, in 1972. Framed in steel and clad in a white concrete aggregate, its gridded face could have been taken as an office building anywhere in the country. The same year Circus Circus, originally a casino, became a full-fledged hotel resort with a fifteen-story room tower.

Fremont Street saw similar growth. The fifteen-story Fremont Hotel, the twenty-six-story Mint tower, and the nine-story Sundance Hotel were joined by the twenty-two-story Union Plaza Hotel by architects Zick and Sharp in 1970. Located on the landmark site at the head of Fremont Street, the Union

♣

CIRCUS CIRCUS SIGN, 1975. THE ORIGINAL ROADSIDE MERRY-GO-ROUND WAS REPLACED WITH A 126-FOOT-TALL CLOWN.

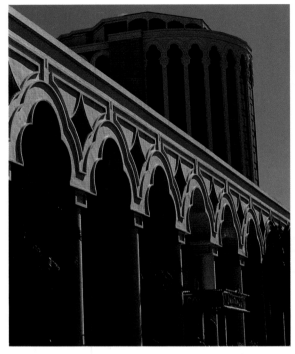

ALADDIN, 1975, LEE LINTON. A DESIGNER WITH ONE OF THE BEST SENSES OF SCALE WORKING IN LAS VEGAS TODAY, LINTON CAN DESIGN ORNAMENT THAT IS BIG ENOUGH TO RELATE TO A HIGH-RISE TOWER, YET SMALL ENOUGH TO RELATE TO A PEDESTRIAN.

Plaza replaced the 1940 Streamline Moderne Union Pacific station; a new train station was included in the hotel. By 1975 the Fremont area was also breaking out of its traditional boundaries, spreading north to Ogden Street when the twelve-story California Hotel owned by the Boyd Group opened. Sam Boyd, who had come to Las Vegas in the 1940s after working on the gambling boats off Los Angeles, became a major casino operator. The Golden Nugget, now owned by Steve Wynn, opened its first hotel wing in 1977.

Strip development also surged past its traditional boundaries and onto side streets after 1970. New hotels or remodeled motels included the Royal Las Vegas (1970) on Convention Center Drive, the Maxim (1972) on East Flamingo, the Palace Station (1976, originally Bingo Palace) on West Sahara, the Barbary Coast (1978), and others. The Showboat on the Boulder Highway added a nine-story tower in 1973 and expanded further in 1975. Sam's Town, named for Sam Boyd, opened farther down the Boulder Highway from the Showboat in 1978; its facade, a collection of rustic false-front buildings, carried on the long-running Old West theme.

The architects were Marnell Corrao Associates.

In the mid-1970s, many gaps were filled in along the Strip. In 1974 the Hacienda expanded its casino and pool, and Jay Sarno sold Circus Circus to William Bennett, a Del Webb executive. Tweaking the ghost of Hughes, Bennett replaced the roadside merry-go-round with a 126-foot-tall clown sign and added another fifteen-story tower and a new porte cochere designed by Lee Linton and YESCO. Following the lead of the MGM, the sign was mostly rear-lit plastic. But the porte cochere was the star. More than any other architect working recently in Las Vegas, Linton retains the well-crafted and exuberant scale of 1950s Las Vegas in today's theme architecture. He had worked for Los Angeles architects Armét and Davis in the 1950s on some of their influential coffee shop designs which mated Modernism and the roadside environment. In the Circus Circus marquee he created an instantly identifiable image of a turn-of-the-century entertainment emporium, scaled it to be visible across the parking lot, and still made its astonishing bulk appear to float overhead. Like most of Las Vegas since the 1970s, the marquee uses theme rather than modern sources, yet retains the daring and delight of the best of the old signs.

The fourteen-story Marina hotel, opened in 1975, incorporated a motel on its site north of the Tropicana. The same year saw the Aladdin add a twenty-story tower designed by architect Lee Linton and a seventy-five-hundred-seat Performing Arts Center. With rounded bays on each end and crowned with superbly overscaled Moorish arches, the Aladdin tower broke the pattern of corporate stodginess. A $250,000 porte cochere, its ornament fabricated by YESCO, continued the tower's arabesques. Nineteen seventy-seven was another boom year with another tower rising at the Flamingo (which was fast running out of land), and a twenty-two-story tower at the formerly lowrise Tropicana (replacing the original tulip fountain). The glitz introduced by the MGM Grand took over the Stardust in 1977 with yet another facade remodeling. The galactic theme was abandoned, though the roadside sign remained, and the facade was covered with animated red-and-blue neon tubing and trimmed with mirrored finish facets. The new porte cochere sparkled with a thousand small incandescent bulbs, too regular to compete with the dazzling roadside sign. This encrustation of bulbs that turned solid mass into ethereal form was a trend continued in the Sands in 1982, where coruscating mushrooms replaced a rather lifeless Modernist porte cochere.

The failing Thunderbird, bought by the Dunes' Major Riddle, reopened as the Silverbird in 1978. In 1982 it would be remodeled and renamed El Rancho, although without any ties to the original El Rancho Vegas.

The Desert Inn took the corporate modern style one step further in its 1978 expansion. Once a casually elegant ranch house, it was transformed into a fourteen-story tower of crystalline facets sheathed in mirrored glass. The imagery suited the upscale clientele that the Desert Inn (comparatively small at 820 rooms) targeted. If the Flamingo's new towers were comparable to speculative office buildings, the Desert Inn borrowed the expensive style of a corporate headquarters. The nine-story tower from 1963 was given the same treatment; even the new roadside sign echoed the mirrored style. Gone was the cloudlike cactus logo. Inside glitzy gold rings hung at different levels from the high casino ceiling. The casino matched the wide lapels and leisure suits of corporate Las Vegas.

Ramada Hotels joined the Hilton and Holiday Inn corporations in Las Vegas when it bought the Tropicana and added another twenty-two-story wing in 1979. Also in 1979, Caesars added a twenty-two-story tower with an Omnimax theater, a golf ball–textured dome, in another appeal to the family trade. Another expansion of Las Vegas' market also could be seen in the 421-space recreational vehicle park opened by Circus Circus on the rear of its property in 1979, as well as the three-story motel wings and a newer, larger porte cochere of 1980. The Hacienda and Sam's Town also added RV parks.

The impact of the MGM sign, and of a new generation of sign artists trained at art schools and carrying MFAs, conspired to dampen the creativity of the newer signs. Typical was the 1975 Aladdin sign. Though the Circus Circus clown showed promise that the rear-lit plastic signs could conjure up fantasy, the Aladdin's new $300,000, 140-foot blockbuster sign by YESCO copied the

♠

DESERT INN, 1978. A NEW TOWER AND A MIRRORED GLASS CURTAIN WALL SWALLOWED ALL REMNANTS OF THE ORIGINAL DESERT INN. THE SIGN AND PORTE COCHERE WERE MANUFACTURED BY THE HEATH SIGN COMPANY.

nearby MGM Grand, with little neon, huge attraction panels, and none of the arabesque of the Aladdin's original sign. While the older signs provided shapely silhouettes against the desert's bright daytime sky, the new signs offered only boxes.

The Flamingo was an exception to the trend to blockier signs. In the mid-1970s the hotel built another new porte cochere that matched the spectacle, if not the height, of the great signs of the 1960s. Pushing this time right up to the sidewalk, the porte cochere sign was a classic of neon and animation, a three-dimensional goblet of pink feathers waving in the neon breeze. A frieze of rear-lit mirrored flamingos—from the new catalog of glitzy materials—strutted above eye level. Both additions were by sign manufacturer Heath & Co. The Flamingo sign/porte cochere, the 1978 Sahara sign (stretching to 228 feet, the tallest of all), and the 1990 Rio sign continued the tradition of the signs of the 1960s.

Then in 1978, Las Vegas' worst nightmare became reality: another state legalized gambling. Since the introduction of the jet, the eastern seaboard had figured as a large market for Las Vegas, but now Atlantic City, New Jersey, threatened to siphon off those customers.

◆

CAESARS PALACE, 1980. THE NEW PORTE COCHERE FABRICATED BY YESCO FOR $300,000 GRACEFULLY DIMINISHES IN SCALE FROM CAR SCALE TO PEDESTRIAN SCALE IMMEDIATELY OVER THE ENTRY DOORS.

BELOW: CAESARS PALACE, 1966, MELVIN GROSSMAN. THE MODERNIZED CLASSICISM OF THE ORIGINAL COLONNADE CONTRASTS WITH THE COPIES OF CLASSICAL STATUES.

This, coupled with a recession in the early 1980s, caused a slump in the number of Las Vegas visitors. Some Las Vegas interests, including Caesars and the Golden Nugget, counterattacked by opening casinos in the rival city. Many of the same architects and designers worked in both cities, bringing a similarity to the architecture. Yet between 1978 and 1983, twelve Las Vegas resorts began or planned major additions, towers, and remodelings.

Caesars Palace, both Hiltons, Circus Circus, Holiday Inn, and the Landmark all expanded. Smaller hotels filled in many of the gaps remaining in the Strip. Vegas World (1979), on Las Vegas Boulevard but inside city limits, painted the entire side of its tower with surreal space stations and astronauts floating in outer space, seen through a screen of the building's pilasters. The Imperial Palace opened on the site of the 1958 Flamingo Capri motel (by Douglas Honnold) in 1980, north of the Flamingo. The MGM Grand's dramatic fire in November 1980 was followed by the opening of a new tower with eight hundred rooms on the south edge of the property the same year. The Hilton burned in 1981, but soon reopened. The Westward Ho motel opened in 1983 near the Stardust. The Dunes Oasis extended the casino out to the heavily trafficked corner of Flamingo and the Strip; like portes cocheres, it was fabricated by a sign company, Ad-Art. This trend blurs even further any division between signage and architecture in Las Vegas. Slots O' Fun, owned by Circus Circus, opened in 1983, when Circus Circus also raised its porte cochere. Several changes in ownership also took place: the MGM Grand became Bally's, Sam Boyd bought the Fremont Hotel, and Fitzgerald's bought the Sundance. In 1983 the Royal American added a paddle wheeler to join those at the Holiday Inn and the Showboat. Atlantic City appeared to have taught more people how to gamble, creating a larger market for Las Vegas.

Over the next twenty years in Las Vegas, towers shot up into the air, parking lots filled in with buildings, and hotels became bigger and more complex, accessorizing sports books with multiple video screens for viewing football games and boxing matches, and adding sports arenas and shopping malls. As new hotel management teams took over and targeted new markets—particularly families—the products became more predictable and similar to the resort products of Miami, Hawaii, and elsewhere.

These changes took a toll on the older architecture. Blockbuster corporate architecture began to elbow out the neon phantasms. Some of the older architecture—the Golden Nugget, the Stardust, and the Dunes—that had seared the neon light of Las Vegas in the world consciousness might remain for a time, but around them rose highrise cliffs that overwhelmed them.

The resort expansions of the 1970s were built on sites rarely master-planned to accommodate such dense growth. Room towers were squeezed as close to the casinos as possible. Towers stood side by side

with two-story motel wings. The palimpsest of styles and sizes and construction techniques gave each resort the dense layering of an ancient city, except that the development of centuries had been telescoped into twenty or thirty years. It was another step in the evolution of the highway into Roadtown, and Roadtown into Strip City.

Then the archetypal Los Angeles will be our Rome and Las Vegas our Florence; and, like the archetypal grain elevator some generations ago, the Flamingo sign will be the model to shock our sensibilities towards a new architecture.

ROBERT VENTURI, DENISE SCOTT BROWN, AND STEVEN IZENOUR, **LEARNING FROM LAS VEGAS**, 1972

The Recent West in Corporate Splendor: 1981–1992

A SENSE OF SHAME entered the populist Eden in the 1980s. The wanton neon of Las Vegas' glittery mobster past unsettled the new corporate titans of the Strip, who often erred on the side of stylistic safety when commissioning new architecture. Some of the greatest icons of American popular culture began to disappear. The magnificent Golden Nugget sign and facade were removed in 1986. The Mint's pink rainbow disappeared by 1988. In 1991 a subdued Helvetica typeface replaced the Stardust sign's Jetsonian lettering. The oasis accented by fountains of neon has become a walled city of red, blue, and green towers illuminated by spotlight.

Enormous theme palaces like the Mirage and Excalibur emerged on the Las Vegas Strip. The balance between signs and architecture shifted again in favor of the architecture as highrise towers dominated the skyline. Masses of new visitors drawn by corporate marketing unexpectedly added pedestrian life to the car-oriented Strip. Density brought an oddly urban character to what once seemed as spacious as the neighborhood A&P lot.

Las Vegas has changed greatly since *Learning from Las Vegas* described it at the height of the classic Strip form. As late as 1978, architecture critic John Pastier noted that "development, though intense, is also loose and scattered." Large tracts of open space, including the site of the original strip resort, El Rancho Vegas, remained. Since then the ranks of small businesses and buildings, common alongside the hotels in previous decades, have been decimated. Today it is almost impossible to

buy gas on the Strip. Motels still stand among the hotels, but in fewer numbers. With the disappearance of gas stations, motels, and rent-a-car agencies, their signs also vanished, reducing the density of signs on certain stretches of the Strip. In 1970, parking lots were vast parterres setting off casino entries, signs, or towers. Today's increased density has been at the expense of many of these asphalt seas, which were considered, as was the native desert, land waiting for development. Free parking can still be had, but you have to drive farther and walk longer to use it. At Caesars, walls surround entire lots, and the parking area is divided into specialized lots for valet, employee, and self-parking, and garage structures. Freewaylike main entries, bypasses, and side entries weave together in a maze.

The architectural changes can be traced to the new corporate presence. Before 1968, only individuals had been allowed to hold gambling licenses. That year a new Nevada law allowed corporations to own casinos, too. In the 1950s and 1960s, an entrepreneur like Wilbur Clark could shape a hotel's look and style, and architects were hired on a handshake. When casinos came under corporate rule, decisions were made by committees. Exceptions remained: after building the International and the MGM Grand (sold to Bally's in 1985), Kirk Kerkorian announced the

♥

HOLIDAY CASINO, 1990, RISSMAN AND RISSMAN ASSOCIATES. PADDLE-WHEEL STEAMBOATS HAVE BEEN A POPULAR THEME FOR THE DESERT METROPOLIS EVER SINCE THE SHOWBOAT CASINO OPENED ON THE BOULDER HIGHWAY IN 1954.

building of a new MGM Grand, another mammoth hotel that began construction in 1992; William Bennett, chairman of Circus Circus, asked for a castle and got one for the Excalibur. But overall, corporate decision making for design issues has narrowed the difference between Las Vegas hotels, and those in other cities.

In 1980 the Dunes built an undistinguished seventeen-story companion to the Diamond of the Dunes. During the 1980s the Flamingo added a string of four look-alike towers by architect Rissman and Rissman which literally overshadowed the old Flamingo; from morning until sundown, the once lush, palm-lined pool built by Siegel was cast into shadow. To save itself from entombment behind these slabs, the neighboring Imperial Palace added nineteen stories in 1988 and built over its porte cochere to firm up its foothold on the Strip. Farther down the Strip, the Hacienda opened an eleven-story addition in 1980 with three hundred rooms.

In the 1960s the voluptuous silhouettes of the great signs of the Sands, Stardust, Frontier, and Flamingo towered over the low casino buildings. The Strip was a city of shapes and colors and animation. During the 1980s, the signs ended their domination of the skyline. From afar the towers dwarfed them. From the midst of the Strip, the signs seemed animated cartoons projected against a screen of hotel room windows. In the 1960s the Landmark, Sands, and Dunes highrises had shared with the signs a shapeliness that made them landmark verticals in a horizontal world. The new towers—the Sahara's 1988 twenty-six-story tower, the Riviera's twenty-four-story tower of the same year, and the 1989 Holiday Inn's thirty-five stories—were flat-roofed and flat-faced and overwhelmed the signs with their sheer bulk. The latest towers, at Excalibur, Sahara, and Circus Circus, are look-alike slabs that reflect mass economics but not mass taste. Windows are square holes punched in the concrete block screen wall. The design finesse of the earliest Sahara and Desert Inn towers has been replaced by brute blocks.

A countertrend surfaced in the late 1980s. Theme architecture was carried to increasingly greater scales. The 1972 Holiday Inn paddle

wheeler sitting on the Strip north of the Flamingo docked a second, larger showboat next to it. In 1990, both were replaced with an even larger five-story showboat. Two more showboats appeared incongruously at Nevada Landing in 1989, a casino and hotel half an hour south of Las Vegas in the middle of the desert in landlocked Jean, Nevada; they sit docked at a replica of San Francisco's Ferry Building. Lee Linton was the architect. More appropriately, the Colorado Belle hotel and casino took the form of a paddle wheeler dry-docked next to the Colorado River in the gambling boomtown of Laughlin, Nevada. The signs of the 1960s concentrated the symbolic function of architecture into single roadside pylons. Now buildings, larger than ever, were being sculpted into symbols.

The historic dichotomy in Las Vegas resorts between Hughesian sophistication and populist extravagance continued into the 1990s with two mammoth new theme resorts opening within a year of

(also the owner of the Golden Nugget), the 108-acre Mirage's three-winged, thirty-story tower is sited well back from the street. Twenty-four-carat gold-tinted glass spangles the white structure.

The Mirage's signboard, on the south side of the property, follows the MGM Grand model: it is a squared-off, flat-topped ladder sign, the grand-daddy of all ladder signs adorning strip shopping centers across the country. It provides information on current headliners and games, but communicates little symbolically and carries none of the neon animation of earlier signs. It was designed by Ad-Art's Charles Barnard, though the simplified concept was the client's.

At 160-feet tall, the Mirage sign is not the tallest sign on the Strip but is certainly the best situated, taking advantage of the point where the old straight-arrow Los Angeles Highway curved to parallel the Union Pacific track arriving in downtown Las Vegas. It is a point on the Strip that has been begging for a landmark, and the Mirage sign makes the most of it; it is a great solution to an urban design opportunity. But the onion-domed Dunes sign is still the greater American art.

At the top of the Mirage sign is a preprinted fabric panel featuring the headliners—usually the disinterested faces of the Mirage's resident stars, Siegfried and Roy with their Peaceable Kingdom. The panel can be changed in a few hours. Below it is a sixteen-color matrix sign which performs like a crude television screen to display simply animated outlines and words. In it, a field of primary-colored light bulbs can be controlled by a computer program to mix and flash, thereby suggesting movement and different colors. Though using high tech, these signs are the latest form of one of the oldest roadside features, the billboard, which in Las Vegas can be traced from the early Strip to the 1958 Stardust facade to these extravaganzas.

In color, light, and action, these animated signs have an embryonic charm which may point the way to a new Las Vegas sign aesthetic. Signs may yet return to the graphics and symbols of the great signs of the 1960s, this time exploiting the infinite variability of a computerized video screen. But for the time being, the symbolism commu-

each other. The $700 million Mirage opened in 1989 on the northern boundary of Caesars, taking over the site of the 1957 Castaways motel, and one of the oldest clubs on the Strip, the Red Rooster Club from the 1940s. In 1990 the $290 million Excalibur opened across the street from the Tropicana.

A national television commercial in 1989 heralded the latest Strip hotel. It showed limousines pulling up in front of a glittering porte cochere; it showed beautifully dressed people; it showed glimpses of flame against the night sky. "The Strip is supposed to be synonymous with a good looking female all dressed up in a very expensive diamond studded evening gown and driving up to a multi-million dollar hotel in a Rolls Royce," Howard Hughes had written to his lieutenants twenty years before. The Mirage fulfilled that image, following in the tradition of Billy Wilkerson and Benjamin Siegel.

Designed by architect Joel Bergman for owner Stephen Wynn

nicating the theme of the Mirage is carried by the resort's three-dimensional theme environment at the Strip's edge.

The South Seas island theme of the Mirage has been concentrated into a compact volcanic island, sitting in a roadside lagoon, surrounded by palms, ferns, and waterfalls. Every fifteen minutes after dark, the volcano erupts in a geyser of steam tinted with red lights. On cue, gas jets in the lagoon spread flame across the water's surface. The informational and symbolic roles of the classic Las Vegas sign have been separated in this attraction.

A large, transparent geodesic dome (coincidentally echoing the Omnimax dome at Caesars next door) near the entry encloses a forest of palms. Thatched huts shelter the main gaming area. Leafy designs pattern the acoustic tile ceiling. The Mirage casino is lighter and brighter than Caesars', but it has the same dense clutter that keeps gamblers focused on gambling. Around the perimeter, glimpses of the palm forest under the dome, or the array of big screen televisions in the sports book, or the French street leading to the finer restaurants encourage visitors to wander. The pool patio, including a dolphin aquarium, is configured with fake rocks into an island motif.

Like Siegel, Clark, and Sarno, Wynn was actively involved in the design and execution of his hotel and was willing to spend large amounts of money to achieve the desired effects. Wynn conceived the idea of a tropical highrise on the Strip, a remarkably incongruous concept to attempt in the middle of a desert. In the creation of fantasy, notes architect Bergman, it is acceptable to completely ignore the natural setting. The contrast with reality makes the fantasy stronger. "We believe a strong theme makes a promise," says Bergman, who worked for Martin Stern, Jr., for over ten years and was project architect for the 1972 MGM Grand, as well as the later MGM Grand in Reno. Since 1979 he has worked for the Golden Nugget as architect, and also designed the Golden Nugget in Atlantic City.

♣

LAS VEGAS BOULEVARD AT FLAMINGO ROAD, 1991. FLAMINGO PLUMES, BARBARY COAST GINGERBREAD, JAPANESE PAGODAS, AND ROMAN TEMPLES SHAPE THE STRIP-SCAPE AT ONE OF ITS BUSIEST CORNERS. THE BARBARY COAST'S GREAT VICTORIAN HOURGLASS MANUFACTURED BY YESCO FURTHER BLURS THE LINE BETWEEN ARCHITECTURE AND SIGN.

The sheer size of the Mirage (over three thousand rooms) encourages populism, despite the hotel's upscale image. The very idea of sophistication has changed since Ben Siegel opened the Flamingo in contrast to the folksy El Rancho. Of course, Siegel's Hollywood sophistication was more casual and democratic than the aristocratic style of Charles Garnier's casino at Monte Carlo in 1879. With visitors wandering in off the Strip today likely to be attired in tank tops and farmer caps than in evening clothes, the Mirage continues the democratization of elegance first seen on the elaborate showboats of the nineteenth century.

At the other end of the Strip stands the worst nightmare of Howard Hughes: the Excalibur. Here honky-tonk and the common man have triumphed. It is the granddaddy of all miniature golf castles, a fairy-tale chateau brilliantly out of all proportion to its surroundings. In a display of executive fiat still possible in corporate Las Vegas, Circus Circus president William Bennett said he wanted a castle and he got one. He sent his architect, Veldon Simpson, on a ten-day, three-hundred-castle tour of Europe; the most outstanding of them was Neuschwanstein in Bavaria. This castle may be as seminal an influence in twentieth-century architecture as were the grain elevators that inspired early twentieth-century Modernism. The same castle also

inspired Walt Disney's designers in creating Sleeping Beauty's castle at Disneyland and later Walt Disney World.

Appropriately Neuschwanstein, built between 1869 and 1881, is not a real castle at all, but a fantasy castle built for the justly nicknamed Mad King Ludwig II of Bavaria, and designed by Georg von Dollmann and Eduard Riedel. Ludwig, inspired by *Lohengrin* and the myths of composer Richard Wagner, borrowed turrets from the Loire Valley, a site fit for Valhalla, and the defensive walls of a real castle. Never meant as a serious fortress, Neuschwanstein has a lightness that real castles could not afford. Real castles are disappointing to the modern imagination; lacking towers for damsels to pine in, they were dank, brooding, scary places and often meant to be so. The fairy-tale castle is just that—a fairy tale.

Theme architecture has more in common with movies than with traditional architecture. This isn't because the Excalibur is like a false-front set in a movie; it is because it is closer to the medium of cinematic storytelling, using lighting, imagery, and sequences to create an evocative setting in which a story ("Our Summer Vacation in Camelot") plays itself out. Theme architecture cannot be judged on its historical authenticity. It creates a new world, mining history for a few building blocks but elaborating on the facts. "It's a different approach to architecture," says Excalibur's architect, Veldon Simpson, "but it does what it's supposed to." Originally from Scottsdale, Simpson has worked in Las Vegas since the early 1970s.

The cues that telegraph Excalibur's "castleness" are turrets, portcullis gates, stone walls, a moat, courtyards, dungeons, and strolling townspeople in medieval dress. "As it turned out, Excalibur didn't look like any of the other [castles]. Mr. Bennett wanted a castle unique to itself, so it has colors not harmonious to a castle. It's a Las Vegas castle," says Simpson.

Excalibur offers a theme environment of erratic quality. From afar it works perfectly. The castle image makes the Excalibur stand out from its competition in national advertising. Seen from the south end of the Strip, the overscaled turrets are a tour de force in the use of scale to defeat distance. It has a magnificent mirage quality in the desert which promises the fulfillment of fantasy. It is an antidote to the bland corpo-

rate office towers Las Vegas had been building for room towers. It reintroduces the shapeliness and fancy of the great signs of the 1960s, only at a much grander scale.

Scale can exaggerate the elements of a building that give clues indicating how big it is. Standard doors are six feet, eight inches high, tall enough to accommodate a person of average height. Windows are proportioned to allow an average person to see through them from eye level. But the same clues can be used to deceive. If a door is reduced in size, the building may appear to be farther away than it is; if a door is blown up proportionately, the building appears nearer. Excalibur takes the turrets and portcullises of a typical castle and increases their size so much that they can be read clearly from far away. The red, blue, and gold turrets are sized so they are not to be dwarfed by the twenty-nine-story towers flanking them; a one-sixteenth-inch model helped to proportion the towers during design. In the interests of fantasy, this sort of architectural deception can be delightful as we see ourselves as Lilliputians or as Gulliver.

Seen up close, however, the Excalibur's illusion begins to break down. "You have to be careful with the scale of something that big. One of the best things about it is it has a setback, but looks like it's on top of you," says the architect. Within fifty or a hundred feet, the turrets disappear into the sky's glare. Park and walk in, and you're wandering along a twenty-nine-story cliff of nondescript motel windows.

The Excalibur concept is rich, but has not been developed sufficiently, though to be fair even Disney had problems creating a suitable interior for Sleeping Beauty's castle in Anaheim. The Excalibur drawbridge plucks people off the corner of Tropicana Road and Las Vegas Boulevard. A variation on Caesars' sidewalk pavilions and moving sidewalks, this entry has none of the trappings of a real drawbridge: no wood planking, no sense of walking precariously over a drawbridge swarming with crocodiles, not even the terrifying thrill that the moat might be cranked up at any moment. Visitors have to walk over to the side and stand on tiptoe to catch a glimpse of the water below, which is completely invisible from the street. Creating a pool that size in the desert is a tremendous effort, a truly Las Vegan reshaping of the landscape for the sake of a whim, and yet it is thrown away because it is so

bridge's penurious design seems like an oversight.

The Excalibur interior is everything a middle-market hotel ought to be in Las Vegas these days: a panorama of a splendid courtyard with turrets, a fountain, and, beyond, a bazaar of colored lights, noise, and activity. The only disappointment is that it is not, after all, a giant's castle inside. It has been scaled down to human size. Yet the interior teeters on the edge of skillful improvisation, which is what it takes to make a castle out of a highrise hotel. The chandeliers are impressively foursquare and medieval, fairly dumb proportions that befit that war-weary era. The circular courts are surrounded by a fake stone wall topped with battlements; above them a sky blue mural effectively brings the outdoors indoors. The chandeliers dangling from the middle of the sky do little to disturb the illusion. This is one of those moments when theme architects realize that the audience is more than willing not to nitpick as long as they get a good show. Arthurian murals in a realist style stretch across walls. "People want fresher colors," says architect Veldon Simpson, so the Excalibur trends away from the dark reds and blacks and low lighting that have been favored by casinos, notably Caesars Palace, and is noticeably brighter than older casinos. The neon ornament capping slot machines and video poker banks—neon knights, swords, horses—make the interior into a carnival midway.

The casino is designed for traffic flow. Architect Simpson, in consultation with the client, began with the pits, the railed areas where poker tables, craps tables, and roulette wheels are grouped. Around this center are placed the "mousetraps": showrooms, hotel registration, restaurant, room towers, escalators, and restrooms that draw people for specific purposes. There is no rigid organization. The purpose of the space is not to make getting from one activity to another easy and clear. Instead the purpose is to release visitors from practicality and envelope them with the sights, sounds, and activities of Las Vegas. The space is designed to get you lost, yet is full of clues. It is not a homogenous universal space. Your vision is filled with tempting activities as you move through the space. Most casinos are a few steps down from the entry, giving a sense of the gambling panorama. Often lounges or bars at the perimeter will also be raised, to afford a place to sit and still be engaged with the activity of the casino. Certain elements are placed or scaled to

♥

CAESARS PALACE, 1972.
CAESARS MARKED THE SIDE-
WALK PORTAL TO ITS FIRST
MOVING SIDEWALK WITH
THIS STYLIZED TEMPLE.

difficult to see. Better the spraying fountains of Caesars Palace that are visible from the Strip and sidewalk.

These details prohibit the visitor from entering fully into the Excalibur's fantasy environment. The idea of walking (or, in this case, being carried by moving sidewalk) from a mundane intersection into the center of a medieval castle is tantalizing, but all that greets the time traveler is white stucco and glaring security lights. The draw-

attract your attention, to give a sense that something interesting is going on over at the edge of vision. Certain areas are lighted more brightly, or the ceiling is taller, or the space is less crowded. At the Excalibur a staircase in the center of the casino leads up to shops and restaurants. At the main entry stairs lead down to a game arcade. This is a space in which you don't have to be aware of what you're doing. It allows you to stumble on new activities. So video poker machines — bright, appealing, tempting — are placed at major intersections as lures to keep traffic moving deeper and deeper into the space. The delightful confusion persuades you to move through the casino, appealing to curiosity more than to intellect and purpose.

The Excalibur design exhibits a brashness not seen in Las Vegas for many years. It is at times innovative: on the southwest corner an entire second entry court with lobby serves only package-tour buses, a major means of transportation to Las Vegas. Rimmed by turrets and scaled to the turning radius of a bus, the entry is fully integrated into the hotel in both function and theme. Yet some of the Excalibur's broad strokes are clumsy. Half the rooms look into the interior court created by the two L-shaped room towers; the view is miserly. For only a few do the turrets frame a view of the desert beyond. Most look out onto the gravel roof, endless rows of windows, and a sunless swimming pool at the bottom.

♠ ♦ ♣ ♥

THE MOST CURIOUS effect of Las Vegas' growth in the 1980s was the merger of two seemingly incompatible worlds. The Strip, designed and built for automobile transport, has developed a lively pedestrian life. Gamblers and spectators wander on foot from casino to casino. This mix of automobile and pedestrian traffic is not completely unknown in the strip tradition; cruising night on any strip in the country always needed

♠

CAESARS PALACE, 1988, MARNELL CORRAO ASSOCIATES. THE ORIGINAL CAESARS STYLIZED CLASSICISM BY SMOOTHING AWAY THE ORNAMENT AND TAPERING THE COLUMNS, BUT BY THE LATE 1980S CAESARS HAD EMBRACED AN ALMOST ARCHAEOLOGICALLY CORRECT CLASSICISM. THIS SIDEWALK PORTAL TO THE SECOND MOVING SIDEWALK TAKES VISITORS PAST A DIORAMA OF ANCIENT ROME.

a crowded sidewalk of pedestrians to admire the passing hot rods.

On some stretches of the Strip, this combination has led to cramped sidewalks. In others, however, architects have responded with imaginative, ad hoc solutions in the commercial vernacular tradition. The corner of Flamingo Road and Las Vegas Boulevard bordered by the Flamingo Hilton, Barbary Coast, Bally's, Dunes, and Caesars Palace draws the crowds of a major downtown intersection. The block from the Barbary Coast at Flamingo Road to the old Nob Hill casino is beginning to take on the character of Fremont Street. The Flamingo lines the sidewalk with plumes of neon, bringing Las Vegas fire down to the level of the pedestrian, bathing the nighttime crowds in neon pink. The neighboring Imperial Palace put in department store display windows, though the merchandise displayed is Liberace's car, piano, and a mannequin—immortality in Las Vegas' terms. At the Holiday puffs of chilled air from the open walls of the casino cool passersby.

These are multimedia sidewalks. Side streets and alleys have developed activity as well.

While some Las Vegas sidewalks are cramped and barren, others are wide and appealing, dotted with trees and signs. The great sign of the Stardust is a campanile to the strip plaza over which it watches. Smaller signs dotting the plaza bring the neon down to human scale. Dancing fountains shoot water from planter to planter. Benches are available. The Excalibur, Dunes, Caesars, and Mirage all add an aural dimension with sidewalk speakers carrying musical fanfares and friendly voices announcing featured attractions.

The most innovative response to the pedestrian has evolved at Caesars. With a casino set 135 feet from the road, Caesars faced the challenge of making itself accessible to pedestrians. The solution was a moving sidewalk that carried visitors one way, from the corner of Flamingo Road and Las Vegas Boulevard up over the parking lot and into the hotel. The first opened in 1972. The solution was not con-

ceived as a solely technological one, however. Marking the entry was a tholos, a circular temple sheltering an overscaled bronze statue of an equestrian Roman.

The strong theme of the hotel has been effectively translated to fit the roadside. In 1986 a second pavilion was planted in the middle of Caesars' sidewalk frontage to serve as a second pedestrian portal. Unlike the first such pavilion, which is in the modernized Classical style of the original hotel, the second is almost archaeologically correct. It goes far beyond Postmodern historicist pastiche to achieve remarkable authenticity. This sidewalk pavilion is also circular, with a porch of columns. Gleaming bronze-colored statues and decoration trim the columns. Mosaics and marbles encrust the structure.

Stepping through heavy vault doors, visitors find a wraparound diorama of ancient Rome before them, setting the stage before they step onto a moving beltway (again one-way) and are carried into the heart of the casino. The pavilion and moving sidewalk are a brilliant improvisational use of theming and technology to overcome the drawbacks of the large parking lot setback, and also to create a vivid public presence at the sidewalk. Caesars is able to maintain the character of a Strip building as a set of dispersed structures, while maintaining a sense of cohesion over great space through the use of themed elements and moving sidewalk technology.

In 1985 a large axial boulevard was laid out to create a second grand entry on the north side of the Caesars complex. Unlike the crowded Flamingo site across the street, Caesars has had sufficient property to expand in a spacious (and grander) manner. The entry also leads to the enlarged sports book at Caesars, featuring twenty-one video screens, one of them nineteen by twenty-six feet. These neo-NASA technospaces, bringing sporting events via satellite from anywhere in the globe, show how Las Vegas designers maximize modern technology in an architectural application. A third entry pavilion with two-way moving sidewalks was added at the northern boundary of the property in 1989 to compete with the newly opened Mirage's sidewalk entry next door.

The Mirage's volcano is the latest example of the thriving sidewalk life. It is the present-day version of the Last Frontier's refreshing roadside pool: an unlikely thing to find in the desert, but worth a look. The Mirage's sign has abdicated the traditional role of the Strip sign as an architectural overture to the casino/hotel. Instead the Mirage has a three-dimensional environment, a palm-laden island where, every fifteen minutes after sundown, a man-made volcano erupts. Think of it as geological audio-animatronics.

An admirer of Walt Disney, Mirage architect Joel Bergman has studied the subtleties of Disneyland's designs in creating spaces where people enjoy themselves. The Mirage's sidewalk has been prepared as a theater for this performance. The sidewalks meander along the edge of the lagoon where, originally, a low berm and plants provided a measure of protection from the traffic behind the viewers. And the people come. It is gauged as much to pedestrian as car traffic, creating a place on the Strip where people can gather as they might to gaze at Christmas windows on Union Square or Fifth Avenue.

Increasing density has added other urban dimensions to the Strip. Once each hotel was safely separated from its neighbor by parking lots and open desert. Today the vivid themed worlds rub elbows and create unexpected juxtapositions. One occurs at the border of the Mirage and Caesars Palace. Aware of the competition for sidewalk customers, both mega-resorts use moving sidewalks to make it easy for visitors to be whisked from sidewalk to casino. At the sidewalk they both position pedestrian-scaled portals announcing their individual themes.

Caesars' is the more elaborate; ostensibly it is a circular pedestal for a mirror-gilt statue of chariot and horses. Flaming urns mark the sacred spot. As at an entry to an ancient catacomb, a few steps lead down inside the drum, and then a moving sidewalk leads up through

♣

CAESARS PALACE AND THE MIRAGE, 1990. ONCE STRIP RESORTS WERE SO FAR APART GAMBLERS DROVE FROM ONE TO THE OTHER. NOW THEY RUB ELBOWS, CREATING UNEXPECTED JUXTAPOSITIONS OF ROMAN ARCHES SET IN A SOUTH SEAS PARADISE.

seven increasingly larger triumphal arches to the top where the entry of the new shopping mall begins. Once visitors step on the moving sidewalks, a sonorous senatorial announcer welcomes them to Caesars with information on the latest attractions. Whereas victorious Caesar rode a chariot through his triumphal arches, these moving sidewalks allow everyman to glide effortlessly into glory. The power of the arch form as a symbolic portal is retained. Water pours around and through it. It offers a glorious spatial experience mating modern urban technology with some of architecture's most durable symbols. It links sidewalk and casino with the appropriate technology and the right touch of imagery. Marnell Corrao Associates are the architects of the most recent Caesars World additions.

The Mirage's portal is an informal thatched hut. It offers a ride through a South Seas lagoon as a friendlier, yuppier voice announces what is in store inside. But through the landscape of waterfalls, palms, and rocks, views of Caesars' seven triumphal arches in Roman Imperial style are visible. The effect is of catching a glimpse of Fantasyland as you ride the Tomorrowland gondola. The images are unrelated except by physical proximity. Yet that juxtaposition creates a new, curious, and stimulating urban mix. Julius Caesar and Fletcher Christian meet at last. It is Las Vegas still at its best, creating a lavish and kinetic space for the

heck of it, succeeding marvelously, and generating new urban forms to bring people
together and move them around. Echoes of
this foreground-background planning scheme
are seen in ordinary strip shopping centers
where fast-food outlets, banks, or flower shops
sit at roadside, fronting for a shopping center
set far back on the parking lot.

♠ ♦ ♣ ♥

FREMONT STREET ALSO grew in density in
the early 1980s. The Las Vegas Club removed
its slender and daring pylon dating to the
1940s and lined its roofline with faux stadium
bleachers to complement the sports theme of
the casino. In 1983, the Sundance Hotel
added a thirty-three-story tower, and the Four
Queens an eighteen-story tower; the Lady
Luck casino followed the trend by becoming a
hotel, adding towers in 1986 and 1989. Also
in 1983 the old El Cortez, a rare remnant of
the 1940s, added a tower to the rear of its lot,
preserving the integrity of its original Spanish-
style building. The Union Plaza at the head of Fremont Street added a
second twenty-six-story tower.

The late 1980s brought drastic changes to Fremont Street.
Undergoing the most drastic theme surgery in Las Vegas history, the
great skeleton frame sign and the red-and-blue neon walls of the
Barbary Coast Golden Nugget were transformed into a Rodeo Drive
boutique with white marble walls, petite canopies, and a modest trim of
incandescent bulbs. The decision was Nugget owner Steve Wynn's, the
architect Fred Doriot. "We thought long and hard about taking it away
and yet it had done its job," explains Mirage architect Joel Bergman.
"Change happens. We like to be in the forefront. It makes us more
attractive to customers."

♥

RIGHT: **FREMONT AND
SECOND STREETS, 1984.**
WITH THE GOLDEN
NUGGET'S VICTORIAN
NEON AND THE
HORSESHOE'S POPULAR
MODERNISM, THE CORNER
OF FREMONT AND SECOND
WAS ONE OF THE GREAT
MOMENTS IN AMERICAN
URBANISM.

LEFT: **FREMONT AND
SECOND STREETS, 1991.**
THE GOLDEN NUGGET
BUILT A NEW FACADE, *SANS
NEON, AVEC PALMS,* IN
RODEO DRIVE STYLE. THE
HORSESHOE HANDLED ITS
EXPANSION DESIGN A BIT
DIFFERENTLY. IT ALSO
DEMOLISHED A LAS VEGAS
ICON, THE MINT'S PINK
SWOOPS, BUT REPLACED
THEM WITH AN EXTENSION
OF ITS OWN 1962 GOOGIE
DOGLEGS AND NEON.

Across the street, the Horseshoe took over the neighboring
Mint in 1988, dooming the great pink swoop. The 1962 doglegs were
stretched all the way down the block and ended with a modified onion-
shaped bullnose by YESCO at the First and Fremont corner. The contrast of signs and images had long been Fremont Street's visual strength;
with the amalgamation of the blocks under single ownership, that vitality
was being sapped.

The expansion continues into the 1990s. The Riviera expanded
its casino out to the sidewalk in 1990. The porte cochere disappeared
into an underground garage. Architect Nikita Zukov incorporated
advertising signs and neon into a whip-curve facade clad with refractive
mirrored glass. The 1990 Rio on Flamingo Road and the Palace Station
on West Sahara Avenue continued the development of off-Strip casinos.
Both were sited close to Interstate 15 interchanges. Even farther off the
Strip, Arizona Charlie's built in 1988 on suburban Decatur Boulevard at
West Charleston Boulevard provided a location convenient to local residents in the developing western sector of the city. North Las Vegas
Boulevard also developed casinos. Until these recent additions, Las
Vegas commercial strips outside the gaming areas have been largely
indistinguishable from those in other Sunbelt cities.

♠ ♦ ♣ ♥

♠

RIVIERA, 1990, NIKITA ZUKOV. BALLOONING ALL THE WAY TO THE ROADSIDE, THE RIVIERA HAD TO BURY ITS PORTE COCHERE UNDERGROUND.

DUNES, 1983. THE OASIS CASINO ALLOWED THE DUNES TO REACH OUT TO PEDESTRIAN TRAFFIC AT THE BUSY CORNER OF FLAMINGO ROAD AND THE STRIP. THOUGH ADORNED WITH NEON PALMS BLOWING IN THE ELECTRIC BREEZE, THE STRUCTURE HAS A SKIN OF BLACK GLASS ECHOING STAID OFFICE BUILDINGS ACROSS THE COUNTRY.

STARDUST, 1984. THE STARDUST'S FOURTH MAJOR FACADE REMODELING FEATURED A GLITTERING PORTE COCHERE INSPIRED BY THE MGM GRAND.

IN THE 1990S theme architecture continued as a major trend. The Hard Rock Cafe announced the building of a new hotel on Paradise Road next to its restaurant. While continuing the Beverly Hills classicism seen in the new Golden Nugget, it will feature a giant guitar sign crashing through the roof and a piano keyboard porte cochere. The Mirage group is building Treasure Island, a pirate theme resort which promises a naval battle on the Strip as an upgrade of the Mirage volcano. Jon Jerde Associates is the consulting architect. Kirk Kerkorian began construction in 1991 on a new MGM Grand Hotel by Veldon Simpson, the largest yet at five thousand rooms. In the 1990s market, any hotel under fifteen hundred rooms is a risky venture. With a sphinxlike MGM Lion crouched at the corner of Tropicana and the Strip, it will turn an adjacent golf course into a theme park based on MGM movies. Circus Circus plans a new pyramid-shaped hotel south of the Excalibur. Las Vegas continues to mirror American culture.

♠ ♦ ♣ ♥

THE CLASSIC STRIP was composed of many elements: recreational, industrial, residential, transient, automotive. Las Vegas' Strip emphasized recreation almost exclusively. It created an entire city district shaped by the activities and images of entertainment. It was a suburb of the Southern California culture of mass entertainment to which Americans increasingly gazed for life-style and urban patterns.

To grow even larger, Las Vegas needed the structure and finances of corporations. The change in ownership dictated a change in approach to design. Consolidation of many small casinos into fewer large ones on Fremont Street was reflected

♦

FREMONT AND FIRST STREETS, 1984. THE PIONEER CLUB SHUCKED ITS ANODIZED ALUMINUM SCREEN FROM THE EARLY 1960S TO RETURN TO ITS OLD WEST ROOTS.

in an urban uniformity; variety suffered. A quest for respectability was reflected in the image of some, while a blatant appeal to popular taste led others into larger clowns, more neon, and more exotic images. These conditions dictated taller towers, bigger casinos, more rooms.

By the 1980s the formative spirit of entrepreneurial experiment that produced such popular art as the Stardust's magnificent 1958 billboard facade had vanished. And yet the commercial vernacular landscape continued to innovate. The denser Strip produced new opportunities to bring people together and to communicate a message. As the Strip became more visually complex over the years, the public also had

grown more visually sophisticated. "We are told that this confused collection of messages is undermining our sanity, but we somehow contrive to find our way through it . . . we have learned how to filter out those communications which don't concern us. We deal with the familiar, recognizable symbols," J. B. Jackson wrote in 1966. By 1990, the American public's custom of channel-surfing through dozens of cable programs had prepared many of them for new rhythms and perceptions. As the Strip became more intense, the public's abilities to comprehend its messages also grew. The Strip was sound and fury, but it signified something to a generation trained by television to decipher an interwoven, fast-paced fabric of symbols, signs, themes, memories, scales, light, and proportion. This is what architecture looks like when it becomes a mass medium.

The Strip remains in the memory as the Superstrip of Superstrips; not just the main drag of Las Vegas but the main drag of the universal supercity of the American dream.

REYNER BANHAM, **LOS ANGELES TIMES MAGAZINE**, 1970

Strip City

AT DUSK EVERY summer evening, people gather along the sidewalk overlooking the lagoon in front of the Mirage. The temperature may still be hovering around one hundred degrees, but they gather with videocams poised. Cars whiz by a few feet away. People chat as they wait. Finally flames erupt from the palm-dotted mountain rising out of the lagoon in front of the spectators. Ersatz lava pours out and boils into the lagoon.

Dramatically, this volcano is no match for Krakatoa. Yet it brings a new symbolic fire to the Strip's neon flames. It vividly demonstrates how the Strip's carscape has incorporated a pedestrianscape.

Las Vegas has long been considered an urban freak. Feverishly devoted to amusement and gambling, it appears at both first and second glance *sui generis*. The words *Las Vegas style* conjure up an inimitable image of neon worship and glitter that has little to do with the workaday cities in which most of us live.

Yet even in the 1960s some observers saw Las Vegas reflecting national trends. "Long after Las Vegas' influence as a gambling heaven has gone, Las Vegas' forms and symbols will be influencing American life. That fantastic skyline! Las Vegas' neon sculpture, its fantastic fifteen-story-high display signs, parabolas, boomerangs, rhomboids, trapezoids and all the rest of it, are already the staple design of the American landscape outside of the oldest parts of the oldest cities. They are all over every suburb, every subdivision, every highway. . . . They are the new landmarks of America, the new guideposts, the new way Americans get their bearings," wrote Tom Wolfe in 1965.

Today it is more and more difficult to view Las Vegas as an anomaly. "Lubbock, Las Vegas, and Los Angeles offer consistent lessons about the form and visual character of cities in the American Southwest," writes Carl Abbott. "They are vernacular environments that have responded to the tastes and demands of middle Americans, with only sporadic and often post facto attention to consciously inclusive planning and urban design." Suburbs find themselves coping with highrises and high densities, with malls as their city centers, and with theme architecture as the primary common denominator. From Silicon Valley to Houston to Atlanta, the sprawling Roadtowns laid out along strips in the 1950s and 1960s are waking up to discover that they are Strip Cities.

These changes have catapulted Las Vegas to the leading edge of American urbanism. Although Las Vegas is not where the strip form originated, it does offer an instructive exaggeration of the causes and effects of a city based on car-culture design principles. With other urbanizing suburbs, it shares the rapid growth of population that brings the stores, restaurants, cultural amenities, and jobs that characterize traditional downtowns. But these suburbs don't look like traditional city centers.

♣

CAESARS PALACE, 1991, MARNELL CORRAO ASSOCIATES. PASSING THROUGH THE MARBLE PORTAL UNDER FLAMING URNS AND GILDED HORSES AT RIGHT, PILGRIMS DESCEND A FEW STAIRS, READY THEMSELVES, AND THEN STEP ONTO A MOVING BELTWAY WHICH CARRIES THEM UP, UP THROUGH SEVEN TRIUMPHAL ARCHES (EACH BIGGER THAN THE LAST) TO GLORY. IT IS AN EXQUISITE MATING OF SPACE, MOVEMENT, AND THEME.

SOUTH STRIP SKYLINE,
1991.
"LAS VEGAS TAKES SOME
ESTABLISHED TRENDS IN
THE LOS ANGELES TOWN-
SCAPE AND PUSHES THEM
TO EXTREMES WHERE THEY
BEGIN TO BECOME ART,
OR POETRY, OR PSYCHIA-
TRY," COMMENTED
REYNER BANHAM.

They are organized on a linear framework and tied to the car. The architecture and planning rules of Grid City, the city of sidewalks and squares, don't apply to Strip City, the city of parking lots and signs.

Strip City bewilders traditional planners and architects. Yet this metamorphosis has happened before. Strip City is only the latest version of the upstart American commercial city. Most cities that are designed by commerce encourage architectural innovation, and are open to criticism. University of Illinois architectural historian Robert Bruegmann writes of Chicago: "Visitors to the Loop in the 1880s and 1890s reported that they found a violently dynamic, ragged, congested, sooty place where virtually unrestrained private capital was erasing the familiar landmarks of the city and replacing them with what were widely regarded as brutally large, uncouth buildings. To cope with this land-scape the great new buildings increasingly became little cities unto themselves, private places that removed their occupants from the noise, congestion, and disorder of the street."

"Dynamic, ragged, congested"—the description also applies to Las Vegas. Chicago's urban upheaval was based on the innovation of steel frame technology that made commercial lofts possible and bal-looned the size of buildings. It stimulated the talents of Louis Sullivan, John Wellborn Root, and Daniel Burnham, and inspired the twentieth-century city. Las Vegas was based on the innovations of the car culture and particularly the motel. Whether or not it has produced a Sullivan, it is thriving just as Chicago did a century before. Writes Bruegmann: "It seems more realistic to accept the fact that, whatever the political and economic climate, whatever the operative planning mechanisms, it has always been the presence of many competing goals, some broad and generous, others narrow and self-serving, that have created our cities. It is only in retrospect that we can appreciate fully how in the late-19th century the activities of individual entrepreneurs in the Loop, without stated common goals or coordination by city planners, coalesced in the development of a new kind of building type and a new kind of city that we now consider a model of cohesiveness."

There is no current consensus that Las Vegas is cohesive, but the other parallels with Chicago one hundred years ago are strong enough to encourage a re-evaluation of the phenomenon of the urban-izing suburb. This phenomenon has been labeled as an Urban Village by Christopher Leinberger and Charles Lockwood in *The Atlantic Monthly* in 1986, who reported that the sprawl of the postwar suburb was only a transition from the old city to a new type of metropolitan area. *Washington Post* reporter Joel Garreau identified it as an Edge City in his 1991 book of the same name. Not all these new urban areas are based on commercial strips. Oakbrook and Schaumburg, Illinois, and Costa Mesa, California, are built around regional malls. Cumberland/Galleria in Atlanta, Georgia, is built around the interchange of two highways. Others are on the sites of industrial parks or farmland. All have a scattering of tall buildings with lowrise development clustered around their bases. All are suburban in character and include business, retail, housing, and entertainment activities. The main projects are developed on large plots to accommodate self-contained office complexes, malls, or auto dealerships. Interspersed among them are smaller buildings for restaurants, gas stations, and small-scale shopping centers. Urban Villages may be as easily defined by what they are not: they are not traditional cities, they are not hemmed in by ghettos or decaying factories, and they are not constrained by the skeleton grid of the old city.

Still in adolescence, many of today's Urban Villages and Edge Cities have only begun to build a cultural infrastructure, the landmarks, symbols, boundaries, and meeting places that help its citizens understand how the city is organized, how to navigate its physical and social avenues, and how to find out what's going on in the broadest sense. In a traditional city, orientation is accomplished by a system of towers and parks, streets and statues, arcades and lobbies, shopping districts and facades, public buildings and private homes. One nascent Urban Village along Great America Parkway in Santa Clara, California, even lacks sidewalks in most areas. Office workers have difficulty getting to a restaurant, let alone deciphering other means of civic communication.

In this arena, Las Vegas becomes a useful model. Though highly specialized, big-sister Las Vegas has been evolving on a fast track that has forced it to experiment with and refine many architectural forms such as the motel and the billboard. It has gained the richness that comes from layer after layer of time. As other urban-suburban teams have done, Fremont Street influenced the Strip, and the Strip, in turn, reshaped the old downtown. Las Vegas also enjoyed budgets more expansive than those of other strips. Though it is true that not all Edge Cities need to have a Caesars Palace or a Mirage volcano, Las Vegas demonstrates how the ancient ingredients of a city—gathering places, monuments, the hierarchy of public spaces, diverse activities, plural tastes—can be accommodated in a strip framework.

The Las Vegas model rearranges the specialized neighborhoods of a traditional city, with shopping, business, and residential districts, into a series of mini-cities, each of which contains all these functions—or, due to the town's resort role, their leisure-time equivalent. The mini-cities are the hotels. Equal but separate, they rarely relate to each other directly. Instead each is plugged into the mainframe, the common public space of the highway. The great signs, the vivid images, the neon and animation integral to this urban form, created an urban aesthetic to make the urban form legible.

Las Vegas is no ideal model, however. Congested and gap-toothed, it contains at least as many negative responses to the strip condition as positive. It doesn't suggest how to ease water shortages, rationalize regional planning, or resolve the myriad pragmatic challenges facing the new suburbia. The Strip, for example, acts as a rush-hour wall between the growing west and east sides of the city, resulting in the same frustrating traffic jams found in other cities. The lessons Las Vegas can teach these new suburbias are not how to solve their weaknesses, but how to creatively use their strengths.

Those strengths are seen in Las Vegas' cultural infrastructure—in the thriving pedestrian life that has grown in the roadside domain of the automobile amd in the workable mini-cities that have been created

♠

THE MIRAGE, 1991. "THE UNROLLING PANORAMA OF FAIRY TOWERS, IDIOT PALACES, MARTIAN MOTELS AND MILE-HIGH SIGNS," MUSED REYNER BANHAM.

inside the resort hotels. Las Vegas has adapted the art of theming to the scale of a city. Exploiting portes cocheres and facades and signs and popular themes, Las Vegas is a profoundly public city. It has perfected the presentation of a public face for the vast space of a Strip City.

Throughout history, from Versailles to Brasília, corralling a loose herd of buildings and landscape spread over great distances has been an urban challenge. In struggling to become a cityscape, many Urban Villages lack a clear public face. They are archipelagoes of individual developments, each office campus or mall ringed with a sea of parking and perimeter roads separating one isle from the next. They look inward. At their best, they provide outdoor space, restaurants, health clubs, or stores and dry cleaners as services for workers and shoppers. The view from the highway, the public realm, is of blandly styled office buildings set far away from the road. Pleasant landscaping may soften the view. Planting and berms are meant to cut off the development from major arteries and freeways. A modest sign and tasteful corporate logo may stand by the highway turn-in, but an urban area constituted of a string of such isolated projects remains centrifugal and ill-defined. Theme parks, not coincidentally, follow a similar pattern.

♦

RIO SIGN, 1990.
THE NEWEST OF
THE GREAT SIGNS,
BY YESCO, FLINGS
NEON CONFETTI AND
SAMBAS THROUGH
A SEQUENCE OF
ANIMATED COLORED
LIGHT.

The average Strip hotel is more practiced in the social arts than most new Urban Villages that turn shyly inward. It makes a point of addressing the street, a courtesy elaborated over the years in the growth of signs and portes cocheres. Strip City inherited this public face from its roadside ancestor, the motel, Strip City's primitive hut. Motels had signs that spoke directly to passersby. As they evolved into the great signs of the Dunes and Stardust, they became urban landmarks, filled with direct and symbolic information, to help people orient themselves. Caesars' moving sidewalks reach out over parking lots to tie the public sidewalk to the "private" casino — privately owned, but still welcoming the general public. Excalibur's porte cochere and moving sidewalks weave car and pedestrian together.

These complexes recall historian Henry-Russell Hitchcock's 1940 prophecy that "were there more really successful motor courts [in Los Angeles], one might hope that the development of a new and widely popular architectural expression waited only upon the development of new functional types." In Las Vegas, Los Angeles' biggest suburb, the potential was fulfilled in ways unsuspected by Hitchcock.

Though untraditional, the great signs and parking lot pavilions are essentially urban because they reach out and strengthen the public arena of the street. This is the Strip's common spatial denominator to which everyone returns after visiting each hotel's mini-world. They have no choice. Adjacent resorts are rarely connected directly to each other. Visitors have to walk across parking lots or drive back onto the Strip to get from one hotel to another. The glittering streetscape confronts travelers with information, symbols, and attractions to help guide their next steps. It is filled with the crowds, competing images, and appeals to pluralist taste (within the Las Vegas spectrum) that are the heart of a city.

Aiding both the public face and private mini-world in Las Vegas is the glue of theme architecture, which defines and distinguishes the sites along the undifferentiated Strip. Theming is no stranger to Las Vegas; this is the city that hired the J. Walter Thompson advertising agency in 1945 to guide its imagery in attracting tourists. The abstract symbolism of the great signs of the 1960s has evolved into the literal themes of the 1980s. They flesh out the linear strip framework.

"Fantasy also has its skills and resources," observed Reyner Banham of the architectural potential of theming. Caesars Palace creates the most thorough alternative world to date. But even Caesars does not equal the totality of design of Disneyland, where almost every view is

♣

NORTH STRIP PANORAMA, 1984. THE SAHARA SIGN IS 228 FEET TALL; THE RIVIERA SIGN 135 FEET. BOTH ARE BY YESCO.

carefully composed and framed, and where earthen berms screen out the messy contradictions of Anaheim. Las Vegas has not achieved this totality. It has not attempted to. Though individual resorts are internally unified by a theme, there is no orchestrated Strip-wide theme. The unplanned juxtapositions of the Mirage and Caesars Palace, for example, visible from each other's domain, add the jarring and stimulating contrast of the South Seas and Imperial Rome. Where Disneyland firmly controls its imagery, Las Vegas' laissez-faire planning allows the unexpected to occur, just as in traditional cities. It is a city with theme elements, not a theme park which is a city. Las Vegas is not, in fact, a Disneyland for adults.

The themes seen today on the Strip parallel, not coincidentally, those at Disneyland as well as in literature, movies, and advertising. These are the long-running myths of our culture: knightly chivalry, adventure among the heathen, the winning of a West, Victorian homesteads, utopian futures, fabulous riches; a mix of lands near and far, times past and future, imagined and remembered, civilized and uncivilized, familiar and strange, real and fabulous, peaceful and violent. At Disneyland they were plotted by one man; in Las Vegas they were evolved by the collective vernacular design process.

Theme architecture has taken the manipulation of cultural

symbols in new directions. We see its effect on new Urban Villages, where a half-timbered Tudoresque restaurant or an adobe-style Mexican restaurant with earthen ramparts sit at the base of no-nonsense glass office towers. Fantasy plays a role in organizing these urban spaces.

The Strip's theme architecture makes it a video screen of the national consciousness. Over the years the range of themes has appealed to a broad section of the American—and international—population. The rustic Old West theme began on dude ranches and spread to Fremont Street, then to El Rancho Vegas in 1941. It is still strongly represented at the Strip's Silver City, Boulder Highway's Sam's Town, Fremont's Pioneer Club, and Arizona Charlie's on suburban Decatur Boulevard. All are, notably, aimed at the local and low-roller market. The Mirage, says Pioneer partner Bill Richardson, "is too high end for some people." Other parts of sinful nineteenth-century American history, including Mississippi showboats and the Gold Rush Barbary Coast, are also still long-playing themes. Nowhere to be seen today, however, is the sophisticated Old West of the original Desert Inn.

The theme of sophistication has continued to have an attraction ever since the Flamingo opened in 1946. The Flamingo was an authentic piece of Hollywood glamour, designed by the architect of Ciro's and the Trocadero and frequented by the stars of Hollywood's golden age. Today's glamour is filtered through the perceived sophistication of Hollywood movie daydreams. The Mirage's plush theme remains largely undimmed when visitors wander through in tank tops and baseball caps, slurping up sophistication by osmosis.

Exotic locales have been popular themes since the Sahara, which conjured up desert locales far removed from southern Nevada. South Seas exoticism showed up in Don the Beachcomber's restaurant at the Sahara, at the Stardust's Aku Aku restaurant, and at the Tropicana, which began with a Caribbean theme but more recently has widened it into a generalized tropical theme with lush pools reminiscent of water parks and two giant South Pacific Easter Island heads (originally seen at the Aku Aku) out on the Strip. The Mirage, also evoking the South Seas, has thatched roofs over the gaming pits, palm leaf patterns incised into the acoustic tiling, a geodesic-domed conservatory with misted air, palms, and other plants, and a volcanic island as its centerpiece on the Strip.

The space-age aesthetic has had a fluctuating popularity, from the Stardust's 1950s Pop Modernism to the Landmark Hotel's futuristic tower. Vegas World alone carries the banner today.

The themes may change over the years, but the constant is this: Las Vegas is a mass medium reflecting the dreams, fantasies, and desires of the American mass culture. A mass medium such as television can change every few weeks to reflect a craze for rap music, or the Persian Gulf War. Las Vegas has maintained the deeper-running themes that remain in cultural currency in American life. In Las Vegas, form follows fantasy.

♠ ♦ ♣ ♥

THE ARID PLAZAS at the heart of many business parks and the half-baked Main Streets of many shopping malls rarely achieve the diversity of activities and the complexity of spaces in the average Strip resort. From the days of El Rancho, however, Las Vegas hotel casinos have attempted to supply on premises everything their guests need to keep them from straying to other casinos. By creating vacation oases with resort shops, pools, tennis, golf, entertainment, and restaurants, the hotels evolved through the years into a small cities.

To understand the character of this mini-city, the reader must first see the translation of a few terms:

casino = plaza
hotel suites = condominiums
lowrise motel rooms = affordable housing
highrises = offices or apartments
showrooms = theaters
pool patio = park
sports book = cineplex
restaurant = restaurant
shops = shops

Renaming the pieces illustrates the prototypical pattern the Strip suggests for high-density, mixed-use development. Las Vegas' mini-worlds contain most of the pieces, in modified form, of a real city. Affordable and upscale housing can be offered close by, as can a large variety of indoor and outdoor recreational activities requiring a concentrated population.

The casino/plaza is a crossroads filled with people and activity, ringed by restaurants, theaters, and outdoor areas, and located within an easy walk of housing and work. The reason it was designed to be central is purely commercial: that's where the hotel makes the most money, and that's where the owners want the customers to spend the most time. And yet their configuration, with a sunken pit overlooked by places to relax and observe, is conducive to a public social space. Casinos are designed to be, to a degree, disorienting. Windowless and filled with an even field of glitter, they have indistinct boundaries and winding corridors. They offer a landscape of delights in which to wander without concern for time or destination. Yet within this distracting environment, there are well-defined cues that guide the visitor to specific places to avoid complete frustration: restaurants, restrooms, showrooms, bars, entertainment. At Caesars the prow of Cleopatra's Barge, a lounge, is unmistakable. At Excalibur the bank of escalators leading to upstairs restaurants is intended as an interior landmark. These cues are designed experientially, not by a rational scheme of right-angled corridors as one might find in an office building. In the older resorts, this spatial complexity is virtually dictated by the layers of additions, revamped entries, remodeled casinos, and new towers deposited by successive remodelings. Like a city, the large hotels have even developed their own suburbs: RV parks at Circus Circus, prize-fighting rings at Caesars, golf courses at the Dunes and Desert Inn. Circus Circus, with its monorail, and Caesars, with its three moving sidewalks, even have their own mini-transit systems.

In a casino the social interaction is focused on entertainment. If the model is applied to developing Edge Cities, it could adapt to social and political functions as well. Such richness and variety are products of the commercial vernacular design process. The function of a casino dictates a space in which people voluntarily stay for long periods, finding all they desire without becoming bored.

Similar design concerns contributed to the evolution, by accretion, of the Greek agora, the Roman forum, and medieval Italian hilltowns, whose scale Caesars Palace approximates. For decades, Italian piazzas have seduced American architects, who have tried to transplant their intimacy, their variety, and their cafes to malls and redevelopment districts. Usually they didn't take root. But an American piazza was evolving all the time right in Strip City.

♠　♦　♣　♥

"To find our symbolism we must go to the suburban edges of the existing city that are symbolically rather than formalistically attractive and represent the aspirations of almost all Americans, including most low-income urban dwellers and most of the silent white majority. Then the archetypal Los Angeles will be our Rome and Las Vegas our Florence; and, like the archetypal grain elevator some generations ago, the Flamingo sign will be the model to shock our sensibilities toward a new architecture," wrote Robert Venturi, Denise Scott Brown, and Steven Izenour at the conclusion of *Learning from Las Vegas* in 1972. Their book challenged the architecture profession to broaden its sources and to look with fresh eyes on the vernacular phenomenon of the strip. The book was initially vilified for taking such a pure example of American commercial culture so seriously;

only later was it accepted as an accurate appraisal.

Las Vegas itself, however, continued to mutate from the classic strip described in *Learning from Las Vegas* to the denser, corporate Strip City of today. Along with other Urban Villages and Edge Cities, it has created a new architecture.

The analogy between Le Corbusier's heroic grain elevator of the 1920s and the 1953 Flamingo sign is still apt. It is as essential to understand the forces that shaped the Flamingo sign as those that shaped the concrete grain elevators if Strip City is to be understood and improved.

The Flamingo sign resembled, in fact, nothing so much as a grain elevator. Grain elevators were also cylindrical and stood on the flat plane of the prairie. They differed in being constructed of massive concrete, an appealingly new, muscular technology at the beginning of the century, finished, if at all, only in the austere gray of concrete or a whitewash. The form, considered a feat of engineering more than of architecture, was utilitarian and eschewed aesthetics and symbolism.

In contrast, the Flamingo sign appeared ethereal and weightless. It was lifted off the ground on legs. The lightness was exaggerated by the neon tubing, glittering in the sun by day and glowing magically by night. In the dark the sign dematerialized completely as bubbles of neon effervesced into the night sky. It was the closest thing to a purely visual image that might be built as solid structure. And yet it was as much a product of its commercial function as the grain elevator. It was meant to be light, pleasing, easily visible to the strip driver. It also had a clear place in a progressive tradition of neon signs stretching from the signs at the 1933 Chicago World's Fair to the 1947 Golden Nugget sign to the 1952 Sands sign.

The major difference between the grain elevator and the Flamingo sign is that symbolism had to be applied to the elevator, whereas it was integral to the sign. Corbusier had to invest the farmer's storehouse with a heroic rhetoric about structural expression and unornamented honesty to make it useful to him as inspiration for a new age. The Flamingo sign, on the other hand, already included symbolism as part of its function. Its designers intended it to be an abstraction of celebratory champagne transformed into animated light and scaled to the highway. It was designed to convey its symbolic message across space.

With the Flamingo sign, the Strip had created, out of its own needs and context, a symbol that shaped and focused space. It was functional in serving a purpose along the roadside. Part of the sign's function was to send a message to a popular audience. Because it already possessed a popular meaning, it was of no use to the high-art world which needed to control and edit its symbols. The Flamingo sign had no shame in being fun, consumerist, excessive, and unconventional. The fact that it already represented a strong aesthetic ideology is one reason Las Vegas has not received attention from the high-art world. The urban form of the strip has evolved the means and vocabulary to communicate a wide range of messages, not limited to advertising messages. This is an essential ingredient of a pluralist city. The Flamingo tower has in fact become the model for a new architecture.

♠   ♦   ♣   ♥

LAS VEGAS IS not an ideal urban model, but it is well worth considering as American urbanism gropes toward a new definition and a new form. The offices, malls, and amusements of urbanizing suburbs are only in their adolescence. Some cities are trying to redesign their old strips into Main Streets. Aberrant at best, folly at worst, those attempts ignore forty years of car culture and its remolding of the city.

As most Urban Villages have only recently emerged from the primal suburban soup, they have not had an opportunity to be remodeled and enriched. The Las Vegas Strip, though no older than many such suburbs, has been changing and remodeling virtually since the doors of El Rancho Vegas opened in 1941. It has been able to evolve many layers, many iterations, since then, giving it a head start over other Strip Cities in coping with the additive nature of these cities.

From Wilshire Boulevard to the Las Vegas Strip, western strips have developed an urban life, a symbiotic relation with the car, a comfortable acquaintance with past and future, and a popular audience. The East and Midwest also had strips, of course, but they were usually addenda to established Grid Cities. Newer western cities grew up with the car, so strips had a greater impact on their urban landscape. Las Vegas was largely incomprehensible to eastern architecture critics, but being ignored

allowed it time to gestate as a city before it was noticed at all.

High-art architecture and criticism did not often help in the understanding of this phenomenon. "In an entirely undirected but diagrammatic fashion," wrote critic Lewis Mumford in a 1962 *Architectural Record*, "Roadtown has automatically grown up along the major highways of America; an incoherent and purposeless urbanoid nonentity, which dribbles over the devastated landscape and destroys the coherent smaller centers of urban or village life that stand in its path. Roadtown is the line of least resistance; the form that every modern city approaches when it forgets the functions and purposes of the city itself and uses modern technology only to sink to a primitive social level." It was, he said, "an anti-city."

"The dominance of the road is reaming out the city and filling up the country, and it may end by making everything one horrid uniformity, wholly disoriented and always on the go," wrote Yale architectural historian Vincent Scully in a 1966 *Holiday*. "Can such a condition support a healthy political and cultural life?"

Other observers were willing to understand instead of to react to the strip. In his perceptive 1956 essay, "Other-directed Houses," J. B. Jackson foresaw both dangers and promise in the relatively young strip form. "Its potentialities for trouble—aesthetic, social, economic—are as great as its potentialities for good, and indeed it is this ambidexterity which gives the highway and its margins so much significance and fascination. . . . One wonders what a Gothic or a Baroque architect would have done to exploit [neon's] theatrical and illusionist possibilities, its capacity to transform not only a building but its immediate environment. . . . One would have to be blind indeed not to respond to the fantastic beauty of any neon lighted strip after dark."

Yet it was Mumford's, not Jackson's, viewpoint that dominated the literature. There was little chance the architecture profession would engage the strip's issues on any level other than condemnation. "It was left to commercial artists in towns like Los Angeles, Las Vegas, and San Diego to create something wild enough and baroque enough to express the new era of motion and mass wealth. There is a terrific Eastern intellectual snobbery about Los Angeles as a city of sprawl, chaos, madness, strangled by the automobile," wrote

Las Vegas is a city designed by accretion, welcoming a pluralist population with a multitude of tastes; a city of information whose signs today place mammoth video screens in the sky; a city based on the strip, a native American urban art form; a city that grew out of the popular and hallowed ground of drive-in movies, drive-in restaurants, car dealerships, gas stations, coffee shops, repair shops, and the road itself. It weaves the car and the pedestrian together, an intricate task that involves delineating safe havens for each, as well as mediating between the vast scale demanded by the car (the large parking lot setbacks and overwhelming signage) and the more intimate distances humans can walk comfortably, willingly and even enjoyably. Commercial strip architecture can be dry and functional, or it can be delightful and exultant.

Today the strip is reaching maturity. The casual linear framework remains, but it is lined with edifices of mainstream corporations, not mom-and-pop hamburger stands. We rightly mourn the loss of the Golden Nugget facade and the Mint's arch, but we can also see that traditions continue to evolve in the exquisitely distorted scale of the cavernous Main Cabin of Lee Linton's Nevada Landing showboat, and in the roadside appeal of the naval battle planned by Steve Wynn, Joel Bergman, and Jon Jerde in the new Treasure Island Hotel. Yet at its heart still lies the simple roadside motel.

Challenges of traffic congestion, water scarcity, and high density are conspiring to draw limits on all strips. But while the strip remained the form of urban experiment, it was at the edge: at the edge of town and the edge of culture and the edge of taste. The strip has been the perfect medium for creating a new type of city where an old city would have been unable to take root. Possessing few natural resources, little unique scenery or parks, Las Vegas was a city that had to be invented— with dams, cheap electricity, defense plants, and the imaginary lines that separate bureaucratic jurisdictions. Those lines through trackless deserts turned a crime in one state into a respected industry in the next. Those lines created a unique and robust economy of amusement. And those imaginary lines materialized in the fanciful silhouettes and neon tracery of Las Vegas architecture. A roadway could become a city. A building could become a sign. In no place at all, someplace could be created. That is Las Vegas' genius.

♥

THE MINT, C. 1984. ONE OF THE GREATEST BLOCKS IN AN AMERICAN CITY EXPLOITS THE ARCHITECTURE OF GLASS AND LIGHT.

Tom Wolfe in a 1969 *Architectural Design*.

Ironically strips were never intended to be cities at all. The home of amusements for teenagers, service for cars and trucks, and restaurants serving travelers, strips originally provided convenient, out-of-sight dumping grounds for the gritty fringes of the car culture. All these functions required large, inexpensive tracts of real estate. The architecture of the strip was expedient.

Yet it is not really surprising that strips should coalesce into cities. They are places where people of all ages and classes gravitate, to see roadside wonders, to see people, to be amused. These are the magnetic forces that make a city out of a set of buildings. Today, when the best seat for a ballgame, a concert, or an election is in front of the TV, the Las Vegas Strip is still a place where people go. It can't be savored via video.

Lost Vegas

Looking south from the Stardust at night into the heart of the Strip, you get the impression of a radioactive Manhattan. It is a unified field of pulsing, shooting, splashing color. But begin to separate out each structure, each image, and the field becomes something much more complex: a telescoped collage of fifty years of American popular culture. The mirrored glass of the Desert Inn is from the 1970s; the Stardust and Frontier signs are from the mid-1960s; the golden Mirage towers and its TV-screen signboard are from the 1980s; the large surface parking lots are remnants of the 1950s; the western imagery of the Silver City dates back to the very birth of the Strip, as does the evocative name of the Desert Inn. Walk into this landscape and explore the hotel mini-worlds and you find fragments of old Las Vegas that help you understand what it once was. Then you can understand what it has become. Ben Siegel's original hotel wing, though threatened, still stands at the Flamingo, and studying it you can discern the casual elegance of the original Flamingo that helped make Las Vegas a success. In the exuberant Stardust sign and the high-style Diamond of the Dunes can be seen the wide variety of talents that contributed to the overall look of Las Vegas.

Las Vegas is the ultimate disposable city, shedding its old skins regularly as it fulfills its role as mirror of popular culture. That makes it a peculiar challenge to historic preservation, which has successfully steered clear of the paradox of preserving these ephemeral structures. The survival of a few old buildings is largely due to benign neglect. Meanwhile, the popularity of new theme environments demonstrates the public's craving for history, even invented history. Maybe, as Reyner Banham said in 1970, "architecture and design, too, have rare wild-life that deserves a touch of creative conservation."

Ephemerality should not be confused with insignificance, however. The surreal beauty of the Golden Nugget's 1950 neon Victoriana and of the Mint's 1957 pink parabolas seared themselves into the popular consciousness worldwide. To remember what they were and why they were is critical to maintaining an awareness of who we are.

It is already too late for many older signs. The electro-jag letters of the Stardust's great sign were replaced in 1991 with a static Helvetica style. The Mint and Golden Nugget signs have been dismantled. Their evocative fragments lie baking in the desert sun, strewn among other signs at the elephant's graveyard of Las Vegas, the back lot of the Young Electric Sign Company.

Though most of the old Las Vegas has disappeared, enough remains for an urban archaeologist to reconstruct in the mind's eye the texture, scale, materials, forms, and imagery of its different eras. The following is a list of original pre-1980 structures and signs that remain in near-original condition as of 1992. They are listed in sequential order, from south to north, to aid readers touring Las Vegas in search of the real thing.

THE STRIP
1948 McCARRAN FIELD: Stone pylons decorated with propellers mark the entry to the original adobe-style McCarran Airport, on Las Vegas Boulevard South one mile south of Hacienda Avenue. It is now the private Hughes Executive Air Terminal.

HACIENDA HOTEL
1944 LITTLE CHURCH OF THE WEST: Originally part of the Last Frontier's Frontier Village, a collection of Old West buildings, this wedding chapel was moved to the Hacienda property, at 3960 Las Vegas Boulevard South, in 1972.

c. 1960 POOL TERRACE: The two-story room wings clustered around the pool give a sense of the spaciousness of Las Vegas resorts in the 1960s.

1957 TROPICANA MOTEL WINGS: The three-story room wings with balconies suggest the scale of Las Vegas in this period.

ALADDIN HOTEL
1962 MOTEL WINGS: Originally built as the Tally Ho motel, these Tudor-style room wings adapted well when the Tally Ho underwent a theme change and emerged as the Aladdin.

1975 HIGHRISE TOWER: The deftly scaled *Thousand and One Nights* ornament offered an alternative to the corporate office boxes that dominated the 1970s. This is one of the few successful themed highrises in Las Vegas.

c. 1960 DENNY'S: Now a souvenir stand sandwiched between the Dunes and a new Denny's, this is an excellent example of the car-oriented California coffee-shop style that influenced Las Vegas architecture in the 1950s and 1960s. The architects, Armét and Davis, were leaders in the style.

DUNES HOTEL
1955 POOL TERRACE AND LOWRISE MOTEL WINGS: Still a good example of the pool terrace as a stage for one of Las Vegas' longest-running shows, people watching.

1964 DUNES HIGHRISE TOWER: The Diamond of the Dunes tower, the Dome of the Sea, and the great sign are all well preserved. Inside, the elevator lobbies with floating stairs suspended on stainless steel rods, the half-inch ceramic tile on walls, the expressionistic fan-shaped canopy on one bar, and other details recall the contributions of 1950s high Modernism to Las Vegas.

1972 MGM GRAND: The towers, porte cochere, and sign of the MGM, owned since 1985 by Bally's, are emblematic of the change in style and scale in Las Vegas after Howard Hughes.

1966 CAESARS PALACE: The fountains and long entry drive bordered by slender Neoclassical arches are original. So is the concave highrise immediately beyond, but the telescoping porte cochere is from 1980. Inside, the oval-shaped casino and the pool terrace are mostly original.

FLAMINGO HOTEL
1946 MOTEL WING: On the east side of the pool stands the original Oregon room wing of the Flamingo. If you edit out the highrises and the pool itself, which is not the original, the relaxed stylishness of Benjamin Siegel's vision can be seen. The railings and ornament of the lobby inside the room wing retain the refined details of the Hollywood Regency style.

1955 MOTEL WINGS: The two-story Arizona and Nevada room wings, designed by Douglas Honnold, are polished examples of the stucco-box motel style.

1967 SIGN: One of the 1967 plume-shaped signs stands on Flamingo Road near Audrie.

c. 1960 DENNY'S: Between the Sands and the Nob Hill casino stands another original googie-style coffee shop by Armét and Davis.

1952 SANDS MOTEL WINGS: Flat walls punctuated by planes and fins around windows and entries typify the elegantly abstract, late moderne architecture of the original Sands.

DESERT INN
c. 1958 DESERT INN SIGN: The Desert Inn Country Club sign at Paradise and Desert Inn roads is a twin to the sign that once stood at roadside along the Strip. It is made of stone and wood.

1978 HIGHRISE TOWER: One of the sleekest of the corporate towers of the mid-1970s.

1967 LAST FRONTIER ROADSIDE SIGN: One of the great signs that defined Las Vegas.

1955 ROYAL NEVADA: Though they are now the south wing of the Stardust, the Royal Nevada's two-story room wings angling around a large pool court memorialize one of Las Vegas' shortest-lived hotels.

STARDUST HOTEL
1958 MOTEL WINGS: The sheer size of Tony Cornero's populist vision can still be sensed in these classic two-story motel wings lined up like boxcars at the freight yard on the rear of the Stardust property.

1964 ROADSIDE SIGN: Undoubtedly one of the great pieces of American art, popular or otherwise. Its animation, crafted in neon and incandescent bulbs, expresses the energy and techno-optimism of America in any era. The sign was unfortunately defaced when the original dynamic electro-jag lettering was replaced in 1991 by anemic Helvetica.

1964 NINE-STORY TOWER: A good example of the modest scale of the first Strip highrises, especially in contrast to the thirty-two-story tower of 1991 behind it.

1964 LANDMARK: Exuberant 1960s expressionism at the corner of Paradise Road and Convention Center Drive.

1969 INTERNATIONAL: Though the hotel is now the Las Vegas Hilton, the sign, porte cochere, and general massing of the tower are original. The wings have been elongated by additions; a break in the window pattern shows the extent of the original tower.

1962 LA CONCHA: More exuberant 1960s expressionism, with a sign to match. Along with the Morocco, Monaco, Days Inn (formerly Imperial 400), Desert Rose, and other motels, La Concha represents a diminishing number of 1950s and 1960s motels scattered among the bigger hotels. The largest concentration, including the Del Rey, Jamaica, Glass Pool Inn, and Royal Oasis Motor Inn, is on the less developed south end of the Strip.

RIVIERA HOTEL
1955 TOWER: Hidden behind the mirrored glass street facade, the original nine-story facade can still be distinguished by long, horizontal strip windows.

c. 1965 SIGN: On the Riviera's Paradise Road frontage, one of its earlier signs can still be seen, an oval with neon upholstery. It originally stood on the Strip.

1950 THUNDERBIRD ROOM WING: This surviving piece of the old Thunderbird is similar to the Flamingo's 1946 room wing. It now sits behind the casino of the current El Rancho, which is across the street from the site of the original 1941 El Rancho Vegas. Incidentally, a neon thunderbird sign virtually identical to the 1948 original sits on the Thunderbird Coffee Shop in Mt. Carmel Junction, 188 miles from Las Vegas in southwestern Utah.

1966 CIRCUS CIRCUS: The pink-and-white tent roof is about all that is visible of the original building, which has been enlarged.

1941 EL RANCHO VEGAS: The site of the original El Rancho Vegas sits vacant, across the street from the Wet 'n' Wild Water Park. Some of the roads once lined with bungalows can still be detected.

SAHARA HOTEL
1952 POOL TERRACE AND ROOM WINGS: A gracious and spacious resort/motel space. If you ignore the highrise backdrop, the pool terrace still has the scale and detail of 1950s Las Vegas.

1959 SIGN: The Sahara's thirty-year-old tri-sided 127-foot roadside sign now stands at Paradise Road and Sahara Avenue. Though it was one of the first that gave Las Vegas its reputation for big signs, its scale appears modest next to the current 228-foot Sahara sign.

SOUTH LAS VEGAS BOULEVARD
North of Sahara Avenue and inside the city line, smaller plots of land generated smaller buildings and a smaller, denser strip compared with the sprawling hotel sites on the main Strip. Several good examples of motels, some dating to the 1930s, can be found in this historic roadside district, including the Del Mar, Holiday, Rancho Anita, and Yucca motels. Several wedding chapels, ranging in style from remodeled bungalows (Hitching Post), to vernacular storefronts (Cupid Wedding Chapel), to remodeled coffee shops (Chapel of Love, originally a Bob's Big Boy designed by Armét and Davis), add to the district.

FREMONT STREET
1941 EL CORTEZ: LOCATED AT SIXTH AND FREMONT STREETS: El Cortez has the feel of old Nevada gambling. Clearly visible is the original 1941 Spanish-style hotel. The first floor is frozen in its 1951 remodel with bezel frame windows and a neon canopy over the sidewalk. Inside the low ceiling, columns, and lack of glitz typify the earlier era.

1956 FREMONT HOTEL TOWER: The intriguing interlocking concrete panels that formed the surface of architect Wayne McAllister's tower are still visible. Though the signage has changed, there are still some original interior details, including stairs and the rooftop terrace.

1932 HOTEL APACHE: Though hidden behind the Horseshoe's 1962 neon facade, the original Hotel Apache still stands today at Second and Fremont streets. Inside, the first floor at Fremont and Second exhibits the low ceilings and compact spatial configuration of sawdust joints of the 1930s. The Mint stood at the corner of Fremont and First streets until the Horseshoe annexed it in the late 1980s.

1951 PIONEER CLUB SIGN (VEGAS VIC): A classic Las Vegas sign.

c. 1965 GOLDEN GATE: A metal screen hides the facade of the old Sal Sagev hotel.

East of downtown, Fremont Street becomes the Boulder Highway, an excellent example of a commercial strip lined with gas stations, shopping centers, motels, and a few casinos. Its architecture includes a catalog of motel history, from motor courts (Chief Motel, Travelers Motel, Rancho Auto Motel, Gables), to western-style motels (Lucky Motel, Ambassador East, Desert Moon, Bonanza Lodge, Paradise Ranch), to classic postwar motels (City Center, Ferguson's Downtown, Starview, Safari, Valley Motel, Roulette, Pair-O-Dice Inn, Sky Ranch), to vernacular creations (Blue Angel), to today's chain motels. As at strips from Santa Monica to Albuquerque to Amarillo and beyond, names and styles here were influenced by the grand motels on the Strip.

BOULDER CITY
c. 1955 LUCKY STRIKE CASINO: Two miners who panned for gold on the marquee of Fremont Street's Lucky Strike Casino in the 1950s are now at the Gold Strike on Highway 93 in Boulder City.

BIBLIOGRAPHY

ABBOTT, CARL. "Southwestern Cityscapes." In *The New Urban America: Growth and Politics in Sunbelt Cities*. Chapel Hill: University of North Carolina Press, 1981.

ARCHITECTURAL RECORD. *Motels, Hotels, Restaurants and Bars*. New York: F. W. Dodge, 1960.

BAKER, GEOFFREY, AND BRUNO FUNARO. *Motels*. New York: Reinhold, 1955.

BANHAM, REYNER. "Las Vegas." *Los Angeles Times West Magazine*, November 8, 1970.

————. *Los Angeles: The Architecture of Four Ecologies*. Baltimore: Penguin Press, 1971.

BARNARD, CHARLES F. *The Magic Sign—The Electric Art/Architecture of Las Vegas*. Cincinnati: S/T Publications, 1992.

BEACH, JOHN, AND JOHN CHASE. "The Stucco Box." *Arts and Architecture*, vol. 3, no. 3, 1984.

BEEBE, LUCIUS. "Las Vegas." *Holiday*, December 1952.

BEST, KATHARINE, AND KATHARINE HILLYER. *Las Vegas: Playtown U.S.A.* New York: D. McKay Co., 1955.

BOORSTIN, DANIEL J. *The Americans: The Democratic Experience*. New York: Random House, Inc., 1973.

BROWN, PATRICIA LEIGH. "By the Seaside, a Splashier Sort of Casino." *Philadelphia Inquirer*, April 1, 1986.

BRUEGMANN, ROBERT. "The New Main Street." *Inland Architect*, November/December 1990.

CASTLEMAN, DEKE. *Las Vegas*. Oakland, Calif.: Compass American Guides, 1991.

CERWINSKE, LAURA. *Tropical Deco: The Architecture and Design of Old Miami Beach*. New York: Rizzoli, 1981.

CHARLES HALL PAGE & ASSOCIATES, INC. *Historic Preservation Inventory & Planning Guidelines: City of Las Vegas*. San Francisco, 1978.

CHASE, JOHN. *Exterior Decoration*. Los Angeles: Hennessey & Ingalls, 1982.

"CLARK'S DESERT INN: THREE AND ONE HALF MILLION DOLLAR RESORT-HOTEL." *Architect and Engineer*, August 1950.

CRAMPTON, C. GREGORY. *The Complete Las Vegas*. Salt Lake City: Peregrine Smith, 1976.

DARY, DAVID. *Cowboy Culture: A Saga of Five Centuries*. New York: Alfred A. Knopf, 1981.

"DESERT INN." *Life*, April 24, 1950.

DROSNIN, MICHAEL. *Citizen Hughes*. New York: Holt, Rinehart & Winston, 1985.

DUNNE, JOHN GREGORY. *Vegas: A Memoir of a Dark Season*. New York: Random House, 1974.

FIELDING, XAN. *The Money Spinner: Monte Carlo and Its Fabled Casino*. Boston: Little, Brown, 1977.

FINDLAY, JOHN. *People of Chance: Gambling in American Society from Jamestown to Las Vegas*. New York: Oxford University Press, 1986.

————. *Magic Lands: Western Landscapes and American Culture After 1940*. Berkeley: University of California Press, 1992.

FREEMAN, ALLEN. "Atlantic City Warily Welcomes a New Industry." *American Institute of Architects Journal*, December 1978.

FRENCH, WILLIAM F. "Don't Say Las Vegas is Short of Suckers!" *Saturday Evening Post*, November 5, 1955.

GARDNER, ERLE STANLEY [A. A. FAIR]. *Spill the Jackpot*. New York: William Morrow, 1941.

GARREAU, JOEL. *Edge City*. New York: Doubleday, 1991.

GARRISON, OMAR. *Howard Hughes in Las Vegas*. New York: Dell Publishing, 1971.

GEBHARD, DAVID, AND HARRIETTE VON BRETON. *L.A. in the Thirties*. Salt Lake City: Peregrine Smith, 1975.

GRAHAM, JEFFERSON. *Vegas: Live and In Person*. New York: Abbeville Press, 1989.

GRATTAN, VIRGINIA L. *Mary Colter: Builder Upon the Red Earth*. Flagstaff, Ariz.: Northland Press, 1980.

HALEVY, JULIAN. "Disneyland and Las Vegas." *The Nation*, June 7, 1958.

HASKELL, DOUGLAS. "Architecture on Routes U.S. 40 and 66." *Architectural Record*, May 1937.

————. "Architecture and Popular Taste." *Architectural Forum*, August 1958.

HATTON, HAP. *Tropical Splendor: An Architectural History of Florida*. New York: Alfred A. Knopf, 1987.

HEIMANN, JIM. *Out with the Stars: Hollywood Nightlife in the Golden Era*. New York: Abbeville Press, 1985.

HENSTELL, BRUCE. *Sunshine and Wealth: Los Angeles in the Twenties and Thirties*. San Francisco: Chronicle Books, 1984.

HESS, ALAN. *Googie: Fifties Coffee Shop Architecture*. San Francisco: Chronicle Books, 1986.

————. "The Origins of McDonald's Golden Arches." *Journal of the Society of Architectural Historians*, March 1986.

————. "Styling the Strip." In *The Car and the City*, edited by Martin Wachs and Margaret Crawford. Ann Arbor: University of Michigan Press, 1992.

HILL, GLADWIN. "Atomic Boomtown in the Desert." *New York Times Magazine*, February 11, 1951.

————. "Klondike in the Desert." *New York Times Magazine*, June 7, 1953.

————. "Las Vegas is More Than the 'Strip'." *New York Times Magazine*, March 16, 1958.

HITCHCOCK, HENRY-RUSSELL. "An Eastern Critic looks at Western Architecture." *California Arts and Architecture*, December 1940.

HUXTABLE, ADA LOUISE. "Peacock Feathers and Pink Plastic." *New York Times*, February 8, 1970.

IZENOUR, STEVEN, AND DAVID A. DASHIELL III. "Relearning from Las Vegas." *Architecture*, October 1991.

JACKSON, JOHN BRINCKERHOFF. *Landscapes*. Amherst: University of Massachusetts Press, 1970.

————. *The Necessity for Ruins*. Amherst: University of Massachusetts Press, 1980.

————. *Discovering the Vernacular Landscape*. New Haven: Yale University Press, 1984.

KAUFMAN, PERRY. "City Boosters, Las Vegas Style." *Journal of the West*, July 1974.

————. "The Best City of Them All: A History of Las Vegas 1930-1960." Ph.D. diss., University of California, Santa Barbara, 1974.

KNEPP, DONN. *Las Vegas: The Entertainment Capital*. Menlo Park, Calif.: Lane Publishing, 1987.

LACEY, ROBERT. *Little Man: Meyer Lansky and the Gangster Life*. New York: Little, Brown, 1991.

LEINBERGER, CHRISTOPHER B., AND CHARLES LOCKWOOD. "How Business is Reshaping America." *The Atlantic Monthly*, October 1986.

LEWIS, OSCAR. *Sagebrush Casinos: The Story of Legal Gambling in Nevada*. New York: Doubleday, 1953.

LIEBLING, A. J. "Our Footloose Correspondents: Action in the Desert." *The New Yorker*, May 13, 1950.

————. "Our Footloose Correspondents: Out Among the Lamisters." *The New Yorker*, March 27, 1954.

LIEBS, CHESTER H. *Main Street to Miracle Mile: American Roadside Architecture*. Boston: Little, Brown, 1985.

MOEHRING, EUGENE P. *Resort City in the Sunbelt: Las Vegas, 1930-1970.* Las Vegas: University of Nevada Press, 1989.

MUMFORD, LEWIS. "Megalopolis as Anti-City." *Architectural Record,* December 1962.

MURRAY, JACK. *Las Vegas: Zoomtown U.S.A.* Phoenix, Ariz.: Lebeau Printing, 1962.

NASATIR, ABRAHAM P., ED. *A French Journalist in the California Gold Rush: The Letters of Etienne Derbec.* Georgetown, Calif.: Talisman Press, 1964.

NEIL, J. MEREDITH. "Las Vegas On My Mind." *Journal of Popular Culture,* fall 1973.

O'DOHERTY, BRIAN. "Highway to Las Vegas." *Art In America,* January/February 1972.

PAHER, STANLEY. *Las Vegas, As it Began—As it Grew.* Las Vegas: Nevada Publications, 1971.

PASTIER, JOHN. "The Architecture of Escapism: Disney World and Las Vegas." *American Institute of Architects Journal,* December 1978.

PEARCE, DICK. "Pleasure Palaces." *Harper's,* February 1955.

PEARL, RALPH. *Las Vegas is My Beat.* Secaucus, N.J.: Lyle Stuart, 1973.

PUZO, MARIO. *Inside Las Vegas.* New York: Grosset & Dunlap, 1976.

RALLI, PAUL. *Nevada Lawyer: A Story of Life and Love in Las Vegas.* Dallas: Mathis, Van Nort, 1946.

———. *Viva Vegas.* Hollywood: House-Warven, 1953.

REBER, WALLY, AND PAUL FEES. *Thomas Molesworth.* Cody, Wyo.: Buffalo Bill Museum, 1989.

REID, ED. *Las Vegas: City Without Clocks.* Englewood Cliffs, N.J.: Prentice Hall, 1961.

REID, ED, AND OVID DEMARIS. *The Green Felt Jungle.* New York: Trident Press, 1963.

ROSKE, RALPH. *Las Vegas: A Desert Paradise.* Tulsa, Okla.: Continental Heritage Press, 1986.

SCULLY, VINCENT. "America's Architectural Nightmare: The Motorized Megalopolis." *Holiday,* March 1966.

STAMOS, GEORGE. "The Great Resorts of Las Vegas: How They Began." *Las Vegas Sun,* biweekly Sunday series, 1979.

STERN, RUDI. *Let There Be Neon.* New York: Harry N. Abrams, 1979.

STOUT, WESLEY. "Nevada's New Reno." *Saturday Evening Post,* October 31, 1942.

SUTTON, HORACE. "Cowboys and Croupiers." *Saturday Review,* March 5, 1960.

THOMPSON, HUNTER S. *Fear and Loathing in Las Vegas.* New York: Random House, 1971.

VENTURI, ROBERT, AND DENISE SCOTT BROWN. "A Significance for A&P Parking Lots, or Learning from Las Vegas." *Architectural Forum,* March 1968.

———. "Ugly Is Beautiful: The Main Street School of Architecture." *The Atlantic Monthly,* April 1973.

VENTURI, ROBERT, DENISE SCOTT BROWN, AND STEVEN IZENOUR. *Learning from Las Vegas.* Cambridge: MIT Press, 1972.

WOLFE, TOM. *The Kandy-Kolored Tangerine-Flake Streamline Baby.* New York: Farrar, Straus & Giroux, 1965.

———. "Electrographic Architecture." *Architectural Design,* July 1969.

WPA GUIDE TO NEVADA, THE SILVER STATE. New York: Hastings House, 1940.

WRIGHT, DOROTHY. "Kermit Wayne: Renaissance Designer from the Golden Age of Las Vegas." *Las Vegas,* June 1986.

WURMAN, RICHARD SAUL. *Las Vegas Access.* New York: AccessPress, 1985.

FILMOGRAPHY

The atmosphere of Las Vegas made it a popular location for many movies. As an unintended side effect, they also helped to document some of the lost buildings, interiors, streets, and signs over the decades. This is a partial list of movies filmed in Las Vegas which make some of these scenes available to the general public. The list includes the movie's date of release, studio, and stars. Though not filmed in Las Vegas, *Bugsy* of 1991 accurately re-created the appearance of the 1946 Flamingo Hotel. In addition, documentary footage from the 1920s and later is available at the University of Nevada, Las Vegas, the Nevada Historical Society, and the Las Vegas News Bureau.

1940   *Las Vegas Nights,* Paramount. Tommy Dorsey Band with Frank Sinatra.

1945   *Heldorado,* Republic. Roy Rogers.

1950   *Dark City,* Paramount. Charlton Heston, Lizabeth Scott.

1952   *The Las Vegas Story,* RKO. Jane Russell, Victor Mature, Vincent Price, Hoagy Carmichael.

1955   *Five Against the House,* Columbia. Kim Novak, Guy Madison.

Las Vegas Shakedown, Allied Artists. Dennis O'Keefe.

1956   *Meet Me in Las Vegas,* MGM. Dan Dailey, Cyd Charisse.

The Werewolf, Columbia. Steven Ritch.

1957   *Amazing Colossal Man,* American International. Glenn Langan.

1960   *Ocean's Eleven,* Warner Bros. Frank Sinatra, Dean Martin, Sammy Davis, Jr., Peter Lawford, Joey Bishop.

1963   *Viva Las Vegas,* MGM. Elvis Presley, Ann-Margret.

1968   *Where It's At,* United Artists. David Janssen.

1969   *They Came to Rob Las Vegas,* Warner Bros. Jack Palance, Lee J. Cobb.

The Only Game in Town, TCF. Elizabeth Taylor, Warren Beatty.

1971   *Diamonds Are Forever,* United Artists. Sean Connery.

1975   *The Gambler,* Paramount. James Caan.

1979   *Electric Horseman,* Columbia. Robert Redford, Jane Fonda.

1988   *Rainman,* United Artists. Dustin Hoffman, Tom Cruise.